Jon Peter Gunnemann
Mission House Seminary
Dec., 1960

A THEOLOGY OF PROCLAMATION

A THEOLOGY OF PROCLAMATION

by Dietrich Ritschl

• JOHN KNOX PRESS
RICHMOND, VIRGINIA

Library of Congress Catalog Card Number: 60-15296

To the memory of my brother
WOLFRAM RITSCHL
whose uncompromising honesty in rejecting
the Christian faith has been a constant help
and challenge to my theological thinking.

Preface

This volume is not designed for those who desire recipes for preaching or ready solutions for the many problems of the preparation and delivery of the sermon. In this sense it is not a book on "homiletics" as traditionally defined. Rather, it is meant to be a study in the basic Biblical and dogmatical questions which, in my opinion, will inevitably come to every responsible preacher when he begins to think seriously about the proclamation of the Church in which he and his congregation have a part. The present volume, therefore, is not only concerned with the Biblical understanding of preaching but also with the Biblical concept of the Church, its worship, and its mission in the world.

Nevertheless, some practical suggestions will be made and discussed, since it will never be possible to separate practical from theological considerations. Legitimate practice in the Church is not only connected with theology; it is theology. Authentic theology, on the other hand, is not only directed toward the practical work, but it is eminently practical and is constantly asked to examine, support, and stimulate the work of all the Christians in the Church.

Since this book is centered upon the thesis that the whole Church is called to participate in the office of proclamation which is held by Jesus Christ alone, the term "co-workers of the preacher" will occur again and again. By this term I mean primarily the session or board of a church. I know from experience, however, that it is difficult to find a church session that is willing to accept its responsibility of sharing with the preacher the task of corporate Bible study and sermon preparation. Nevertheless, it is possible to begin this hard work of finding responsible co-workers by inviting youth groups to assist the minister in the first part of his sermon preparation. If even this should prove impossible, the first step toward this necessary development will be to preach consistently on those Bible passages which have been studied in one of the study groups of the congregation on the preceding Sunday. This is what I am doing at the moment in a small preaching station in order to guarantee at least a connection between the work of the congregation and the work of the preacher. It is obvious, of course, that the last and decisive part of the sermon preparation will be the minister's own work, however helpful the co-operation of the congregation might have been. It is at this point that every preacher is asked to give his utmost and never try to save time for other work in the Church.

The reader may appreciate knowing why I have written this book. When I left the pastorate I felt that the transition to the teaching ministry would be easier and more fruitful if I spent some years of special study in one of the two main fields of pastoral activity: preaching and counseling. I decided in favor of the former and tried to rethink and formulate *why* the Church is called to preach and *what* we are actually doing when we preach. The fact that I am not interested in the question of *how* to preach may be due partly to my theological background and partly also to the practical experiences which I had in Europe. My own attempt at preaching in two languages and in various countries on both sides of the "Iron Curtain" has strengthened my negative feelings toward any technical recipes or "practical homiletics." The content is what matters; form and technique will grow out of the content, not vice versa. To preach exclusively on the basis of a Biblical text—as long as we are in this world, and not yet in the "heavenly city" without a temple—is surely not a matter of "technique," but the very condition of all authentic preaching. Where would the Confessional Church have been during the Hitler period, and where would the churches be in their present difficulties, if the preachers presented "subjects" and "topics"? And where will the Church on the American scene be if its preachers continue to do this?

I may also mention that when writing these pages I was tempted to take issue with the school of Rudolf Bultmann and to discuss the new hermeneutical methods presented by some of its adherents (Ernst Fuchs and others). I had to forego this; but the theologically trained reader will detect a kind of silent discussion with some influential theologians of our day.

For the sake of clarification, I would add that I am using the terms "dogmatics" or "dogmatical" in the sense of the American usage of "systematic theology" or "theological," and the terms "theology" or "theological" as embracing the whole thinking task of the Church, *all* of the "subjects" which the ministerial student or minister must study.

Before writing this book I prepared a shorter study on some of the points that seemed important to me and sent it to friends here and abroad in order to hear their criticisms and suggestions. After having rewritten it several times I felt ready to prepare this book. The preliminary study has appeared in German under the title *Die homiletische Funktion der Gemeinde,* as No. 59 of *Theologische Studien.*

I would take this opportunity of thanking the many friends who have supported me with their help and encouragement. Besides my colleagues and many ministers from whom I learned a great deal in discussion groups and seminars on preaching, I would particularly mention my friend and colleague in the Old Testament, Professor James A. Wharton, who made many valuable suggestions, and the Rev. Arthur H. Williams, Jr., my former student assistant, without whose help and patience with my use of the English language the writing of this book would not have been possible.

Austin Presbyterian   Dietrich Ritschl
Theological Seminary

Contents

As often as the Word of God is preached, it makes men's consciences before God happy, broad, and certain, because it is a word of grace and forgiveness, a good and beneficial word. As often as the word of man is preached, it makes men's consciences in themselves sad, narrow, and anxious, because it is a word of law, wrath, and sin pointing to what man has not done and all that he ought to do.

(Quoties verbum dei praedicatur, reddit laetas, latas, securas conscientias in deum, quia est verbum gratiae, remissionis, bonum et suave, quoties verbum hominis, reddit tristem, angustam, trepidam conscientiam in seipsa, quia est verbum legis, irae et peccati, ostendens, quid non foecerit, et quanta debeat.)

(Martin Luther)

Introduction

1. THE DECEIT OF PREACHING

The understanding of the Church's proclamation is in all its parts intimately connected with Christology, since it is the living Christ who is being preached. It is, therefore, the endeavor of this book to take this relationship seriously, with all its implications.

It necessarily follows from this relationship that the sermon is endangered from two sides which are analogous to the two main heresies in Christology. The sermon can be understood as the attempt to lift the members of the congregation from their sin and lack of faith to the liberating heights of the knowledge of Christ by appealing to their willingness to believe and to be saved. This—the ideal of the "conversion preachers"—corresponds to the Ebionite or adoptionist heresy. In opposition to this, however, the sermon can also be understood as the task of bringing the glory of the divine truth down into the depths and misery of the human situation. This—the ideal of the exponents of theories concerning "communication"—corresponds to the docetic heresy. Though these two positions are in principle opposed, it is by no means impossible that one can become the victim of both these errors at the same time.

In addition to these two principal errors, the sermon is also endangered from two sides stemming from the understanding of the function of the minister and the ability of the congregation. First, there is the "foolishness of preaching" as a cheap concept which can be used as an excuse. We can admit that last week's sermon did not meet success and yet we can say so without shame. That is, we can be dishonest with ourselves and merciless to the congregation. In this way we accuse the content of the Biblical message of being that "foolishness" or "stumbling block"

which was the foolishness of our own preaching, and therefore
it is an unreal stumbling block for the congregation. Thus our
own lack of wisdom would wrongly be taken as the "foolishness
of God."

There is, secondly, the danger each week that we preachers
despairingly feel that no one will believe our message. Then the
question of Isaiah 53:1, "Who has believed what we have heard?",
will be much more important than the question: How do I preach?
For the second question we have found comfort either in seriously
elaborated answers or in superficially accepted routines. But the
question remains: "Who has believed what we have heard?"
(See also Romans 10:16.) And we are tempted to ask the absurd
question: How can I make "relevant" what I want to say?

The preacher is depressed when he realizes that the congregation will not believe his sermon, that the message will not be
accepted, that nothing grows and that no result is to be seen. It
is much more alarming, however, when the congregation, or some
members of it, will "believe" our sermon, or take us at our word.
What have we done! "Let not many of you become teachers,
my brethren, for you know that we who teach shall be judged
with greater strictness." (James 3:1.) And in verse 5, it is said
of the tongue, "How great a forest is set ablaze by a small fire!"

Reinhold Niebuhr, in his book *Beyond Tragedy*, has published
a meditation on the sentence, "As deceivers, and yet true." (2
Corinthians 6:8, King James Version.) But the terrible tension
in which the preacher and the congregation find themselves is
even there described too peacefully and depicted in an abstract
manner. It is taken as a "dialectical" tension, and therefore it does
not appear to be so bad. There are two extremes to be avoided.
We do not want to use "religious blackmail," which is the false,
"ignoble," and "unchristian" effort "to exploit the weakness of man
for purposes alien to him and not freely subscribed to by him."[1]
Nor do we want to use the pious repetition of formulas and Bible
verses. But even if we thought we had found the knife-edge to

---

[1] Dietrich Bonhoeffer, *Prisoner for God,* Letters and Papers from Prison
(New York: The Macmillan Company, 1953), p. 147.

walk between these extremes, and that we could walk in safety every Sunday—even then we could not escape the judgment. It is "as if a man fled from a lion, and a bear met him; or went into the house and leaned with his hand against the wall, and a serpent bit him." (Amos 5:19.)

"We cannot do what we want to do and we cannot attain what we should like to attain. This is the . . . law under which all Church proclamation without exception stands."[2]

In spite of this fact, should it not be possible to find a way out of this dilemma, to construct a good theological thought? Gustaf Wingren in his new book[3] attempts to find such an easy way out by pointing to the priority of the Word and the unity of subject and object in Jesus Christ. But in spite of all such good thoughts, do we not depend utterly on God's promise that he will surprise us and will do in the assembled congregation what we could never do?

Can we not see this fact in our own experience as preachers? Each one of us prepares his sermon in a characteristic way. Some of us begin on Monday, others Saturday night. Some of us allow much time for a long breakfast, and others will not feel able to do that. No specific and binding rules can be given which apply to the technical preparation of the sermon. But there is one experience we all have in common: when we think that we "got our message across" and have preached a solid and wonderful sermon, often not even our closest friends will indicate that they have heard the voice of the living Lord. And, on the contrary, when we left the pulpit completely depressed and were determined to change our whole preaching technique and even to leave the ministry, we can often recognize that the living Lord has spoken and has been heard.

Part of the cruelty (which we ourselves have created) of our Church is that minister and congregation are separated in such a way that the preacher is alone and isolated with his preaching

[2] Karl Barth, *Church Dogmatics*, Vol. I, Part 2 (New York: Charles Scribner's Sons, 1956), p. 750.
[3] *Die Predigt* (Göttingen: Vandenhoeck and Ruprecht, 1955). Translation from Swedish.

task. He has to try during the hour of the Sunday service to do all that which was left undone during the week: a true contact with his people, a real mutual understanding, an honest spiritual authority, a correct didache, a prayer together, a sober adoration and most of all the proclamation. All these burdens are on his own shoulders. He really is humiliated. If kind people tell their minister that he has a difficult life, they say something which is correct and at the same time neutral. The real burden and cost of discipleship is not defined by this statement. By analogy, the intellectual who says that the minister cannot "speak about God" is also right, but he does not really know why. Indeed, we cannot carry the burden of our preaching task, nor can we speak about God. The real human impossibility of preaching and of talking about God can only be seen on grounds of the divine command to preach. Only on the grounds of the commission to preach—"Woe to me if I do not preach the gospel!" (1 Corinthians 9:16)—can the real burden of the minister be understood. "If I say, 'I will not mention him, or speak any more in his name,' there is in my heart as it were a burning fire shut up in my bones, and I am weary with holding it in, and I cannot." (Jeremiah 20:9; see also Acts 4:20.)

Is it possible, then for the congregation to share at least a part of the burden of the minister? Is it possible to share this burden without minimizing the special function of the minister? This question is one of the subjects of this book. There is probably no minister who has been spared the experience that not even his best friends and relatives could help him at those times that he needed help the most. And secretly each minister will know that this is good. Nevertheless, we must be very careful to distinguish sharply between the real burden and duty of the minister, which cannot be shared with others, and the self-imposed burdens and tasks which can very well be transferred to the congregation. Here we must even say that if this does not happen, if the minister always lives and works within the bounds of our "Protestant individualism," then we will inevitably be the victims of the confusion between the real cost of discipleship and the unreal *skandalon.* The true following of Christ will be confused with the false usurpation of the minister's duties. Such confusion will also be seen in the minister's sermons (and who is completely free of this confusion?), and the congregation on Sunday will be confronted with a "foolishness" of the sermon which ought not to be foolishness at all.

The bewilderment about preaching is, therefore, related to our confusion about the conception of the ministry. Our uncertainty about the position of the minister is connected with our unsettled views of the form of worship, but more especially with our difficulties of understanding the relation between the Church and the world. For this reason D. T. Niles says, "We have lost contact with the world."[4] And we can easily see why this is true: our preaching as well as our liturgy, including our church music, is primarily performed in the forms of the nineteenth century. The structure of preaching and worship in the Early Church and in the time of the Reformation is obscured by the nineteenth-century thought patterns, so that it can hardly be recognized. We have lost sight of the direct connection with the roots of our traditions, and we do not even feel secure enough to judge clearly whether this or that method is false or heretical. The variety of denominations, in which different answers are given to the same questions, makes this confusion quite evident.

These difficulties are indeed connected with the fact that we are still in this world, and that we are not yet redeemed and living in heaven, singing with the angels. We constantly work with the danger of being misunderstood, and even of not understanding for ourselves what we want others to understand. Therefore, the sermon makes the one who preaches small and unimportant. He cannot leave the pulpit with the feeling that he is the man who knows and who has proved how the message should be preached. We must preach and yet we cannot demonstrate or prove. We must even realize that our best sermons necessarily require another sermon next Sunday, since we cannot

[4] *Preaching the Gospel of the Resurrection* (Philadelphia: The Westminster Press, 1953), p. 87.

once and for all give the Word of life to our people. We cannot
speak as "great preachers" as if the word of a "great preacher"
were more valid than that of an unknown minister, and as if
another sermon were not needed. "Great preachers" existed only
in the minds of pious people in the nineteenth century.

There are many suggestions or recipes which propose to lead
to a better understanding of the conception of the function of
the minister and his preaching task. Many answers to the problem
have been given in homiletical literature. Strong movements in
the Churches, in Europe as well as in America, try to provide
solutions for the dilemma of preaching. The liturgical movement
demands more adoration; certain groups ask for a closer connection between the Sunday sermon and house visitations in the
parish; others call for community life and the setting up of community centers; and still others trust better theology and techniques of homiletics. All the movements can be divided into two
groups. One concentrates on the task of the minister and tries
to teach him how to improve his position. The other is interested
in the congregation and tries to teach the church-going people
how to read their Bibles, to understand the sermon, and to share
in the responsibility of the minister. It is not surprising that many
more books of the first category are published, since it is far
easier to reach and instruct students and ministers than to teach
and to persuade church members.

A call for help, therefore, is extended by many writers of homiletical literature to the wisdom of the disciplines of pastoral
theology, psychology, group dynamics, and even rhetoric. But
it would appear that in all these approaches two main problems
are omitted. Besides the fact that dogmatics in this connection
is almost always despised as something "dead" and abstract, the
first group of questions which is neglected is: Who is the bearer
of the responsibility for the proclamation? If it is Jesus Christ
Himself who is ultimately responsible for the proclamation in His
Church, who is penultimately responsible? How is it possible
that men can speak the Word of God? The second complex of
questions is: Since homiletical literature normally talks about

"the" sermon and deals with "the" Sunday worship, as if these events were not repeated, should not one rather try to think about fifty-two or more sermons as the regular and normal work in the life of the Church, i.e., as a motion picture and not a still photograph? How is the continuity of the life in the Church related to the actual and concrete call of the Word of God?

This book will center around these two groups of questions. Since the first of them is the object of dogmatics, it has unfortunately not yet found a home in the homiletical endeavors of our Church and has, therefore, no real profile. It is a fundamental question of homiletics and cannot possibly be separated from it. If we would not falsely separate dogmatics from homiletics, we would see more clearly the answer to the second question also.

Often our thinking about preaching is split into two extremes which are poles apart from each other. In the Biblical and dogmatical work of the ecumenical Church many new possibilities have been opened up which are still not used for homiletical work. However, the preachers are struggling with their own "practical" conception of preaching and reconstructing out of this conception their "own dogmatics." There is no doubt but that all thinking and working on preaching and all statements about preaching are dogmatical statements. The only question is whether the dogmatics is Biblical or not. Even a completely untrained sectarian preacher is inevitably a systematic theologian. And even the statement that "dogmatics is not necessary," is a dogmatical statement. It should, therefore, be clear that the Biblical and dogmatical work of the Fathers and the Church of our time must be known by the man who undertakes the task of preaching.

2. THE GLORY OF PREACHING

Not only is it easy to talk and to write about the dilemma of the sermon; it is even comparatively easy for theologians, as well

as for church members in general, to analyse the possible reasons
for the difficulties and dilemmas of preaching. It has always been
possible to see and to say what is wrong with the Church, where
the Church fails, and why the responsible men in the Church do
not succeed in their task.

How should we learn to understand now the glory and power
of preaching? How can we rejoice in that God says his Word
"shall not return to me empty, but it shall accomplish that which
I purpose"? (Isaiah 55:11.) How can we concretely experience
that God's Word is "like a hammer" (Jeremiah 23:29) and that
the preaching of the cross is "the power of God" (1 Corinthians
1:18)? The answer should be clear: we cannot reach this understanding by theoretical investigation, nor can a theological system lead us to the realization of this power. We cannot define
the sermon (or the "essence of the sermon"). We can only *listen*
to a sermon. "So faith comes from what is heard, and what is
heard comes by the preaching of Christ." (Romans 10:17.) The
very content of the sermon enables us to understand what a
sermon is and commissions us to preach a sermon. This sounds
illogical, but it is Biblical logic. Therefore, it is impossible for us
to think about a sermon as if it were a work of art, as if we
could control, structure, and mold it according to our own theological thinking. If it is true that the sermon is the living Word
in which Jesus Christ, the only true Preacher, wants to proclaim
Himself, then it is also true that the living Word cannot depend
on us, but that we depend on the Word. "The transcendent
power" is of God, and not of us. (2 Corinthians 4:7.) The preacher
must listen and pray before he can structure his thoughts and
before he preaches. He is forced to preach, "for necessity is laid
upon me." (1 Corinthians 9:16.) He is not ultimately responsible
for his sermon, but God is responsible for his ministry and,
therefore, also for his sermon. This is the only reason that we
can speak of the power and glory of preaching.

Not only the most dangerous, but above all the most wonderful, thing which can happen among men is that human beings in
all their disobedience and ignorance can be used to preach the

good news of God in Christ. Men can speak the Word of life. Their witness can change hearts and create lives. The Word of the living Lord can really be heard in the sermon: "I who speak to you am he." (John 4:26.) The man who preaches in this way, the true Biblical preacher, can even see fruit and receive gratitude from those who have heard the words of life from his mouth. This is the beginning of his genuine authority in the Church among the believers; he can become the "father in faith" for many of them. The preacher himself will be cleansed and forgiven. He himself will be a new man. He will not preach because he is a new man—what would happen if we wanted to rely on this?—but the very sermon he preaches will make him a new creation, just as it gives the bread of life to the congregation.

This trust in the power of the word of preaching as the Lord's own Word should be noticed in all our Sunday sermons. A sermon has to be positive, or else it is not a sermon. Every sermon must express the gracious will of God in Christ Jesus to be in solidarity with sinners. If the sermon does not say that God loves those who do not love Him, it might be called a sermon of the synagogue, but it is surely not a sermon of the Christian Church. The sermon offers what the world cannot offer. It offers what God offers. God gives away His secret; He gives His love and His life. This is what is called "revelation." God reveals Himself. The sermon participates in the revelation. This is a dangerous statement, and yet it is precisely what the Bible calls our commission to preach. The glory of the sermon is not ours, but ours is the commission to preach. The power of the sermon is not ours, but ours is the invitation to listen.

The Word, which is Jesus Christ, shall perform its own work. Therefore it must be said that the sermon will not only create individually life and faith, but it will also determine the history of the world. The proclamation of the will of God does not depend upon the situation and history of the world. Preachers must not depend upon their analysis of the world to decide what to preach. They must not analyse people before they confront

them with the living Word.[5] That which is still hidden to our eyes
will soon be made visible: that every knee shall bow down and
every tongue shall confess that Jesus Christ is Lord. The Gospel
of Christ is not a religion, nor is it an ideology. It cannot be
"spread out" as philosophies and ideologies are spread out by
means of persuasion, teaching, propaganda, or force. Mission
work in the name of Christ is harvest work. When the missionary
comes to godless places and Godforsaken people in this world,
he will find Jesus Christ already at work. Christ does not receive
"converts" from our hands. When we preach and give witness, we
receive people from His hands. Preaching is not dispensing
power or giving something to people, but preaching is receiving
power and collecting and gathering people. "Lift up your eyes,
and see how the fields are already white for harvest." (John
4:35.) We are not to convert others, but we have to convert
ourselves to others.[6] That would in fact be preaching and teaching
the nations to follow Christ. The wall between the Church and
the world has been torn down by the work of Jesus Christ.[7] We
can do our preaching and teaching in a way that is independent
of the religions and ideologies of the countries we live in and
irrespective of the social structures of East and West. Our preaching should not deny or deliberately destroy the world, but our
words, as words of life and death, should preach Jesus Christ, who
is at work in this world because He loves it. The hope for His
return in power and for the visible breaking in of the new world
will make it possible for the preachers in our time to do their
work joyfully; not in a hurry, but in expectancy; not under pressure, but under God's commandment and protection.

Are these statements too optimistic and idealistic? They are
indeed unrealistic so long as we do not see that Jesus Christ
Himself is the true Preacher and Evangelist who makes Himself

[5] For Paul Tillich's "analysis of the human situation" and method of
correlation, see footnote on p. 179.
[6] I owe this formulation to Christian Maurer, *Evangelische Predigt Heute*
(Moers: Verlag Neukirchen, 1957), p. 30.
[7] Cf. Markus Barth's commentary on Ephesians, *The Broken Wall* (Philadelphia: The Judson Press, 1959), pp. 39 ff.

relevant, and that He is acting with His people when they preach in His name. Jesus Christ is not the object of our sermons, but rather He is primarily the subject of our preaching. He is acting. We are being used, and we are the object of His words. If this were not true, then, of course, we could neither see nor speak of the "glory of preaching."

I The Word to the Church and the Word from the Church

1. THE THREE FORMS OF THE WORD

The Word of God in its preached, written, and revealed forms cannot be thought of apart from God the Holy Spirit, God the Son, and God the Father. The "first form of the Word," the proclamation, is the peculiar work of the Holy Spirit, through whom the Church hears and preaches the revelation of God in Christ.

Jesus did not write a book, and this fact is not without significance. He, the living Word of God, was made flesh. He was not made a book. The books of the Bible were written by those who gave witness to the living Word. The Old Testament gives witness to the coming Lord. It is a book of expectancy and hope, a book that demands fulfillment. The New Testament gives witness to the Lord who has come, to His Incarnation, Crucifixion, and Resurrection. It is a book of fulfillment and perfection. And yet it opens our eyes to the hope of final fulfillment at the last day, the Second Advent.

While all the books of the Old and of the New Testament contain "words," we speak of the "Biblical Word." All these words present either God's words to men, or men's words to God; either God's actions with His people, or people's actions with their God. In the midst of these Biblical words is the living Word, God Himself in Jesus Christ. In Christ, God acted and spoke at the same time. Here we see that God's speaking and God's acting cannot be separated from each other. However, we cannot do what God can do. When God speaks, He creates. By uttering words He created the world. We cannot do this. When we want to create something, we must first of all think and plan, then we must work and create, and later on we can perhaps "talk" about it, i.e., make "words" about our actions. If a man speaks before he acts and works, people laugh at him. This raises a problem for preaching: Whose words are we speaking when we preach?

This problem is discussed in philosophical terms as the "subject-object" relation. In theological terms it is known as the problem of the relation between the Word of God and the word of man. We are confronted with this so-called "subject-object split" at least every Sunday. Who speaks in our worship services, God or men or both? If both, can we define specific parts of our services as "divine" words, e.g., the Scripture reading and the sermon, and others as "human" words, e.g., the prayers and hymns? Would not this be a very artificial distinction? And in addition, is it really true to say that a prayer is "only a human" word? We read in Romans 8:26 that "the Spirit himself intercedes for us with sighs too deep for words." Hence it seems possible to say that even our prayers are not merely our human words. How much more would that be true for the sermon! For we read in Jeremiah 1:9, "Behold, I have put my words in your mouth," and Luke 10:16, "He who hears you hears me, and he who rejects you rejects me." However, in spite of these promises, we speak about "poor sermons," we talk about "making" a sermon, and we "train" students to be "good preachers." How can all this be justified, if the sermon "is" the Word of God?

In order to understand the roots of this problem, we must ask what "the Word" actually is. We must ask the question whether there are really two types of words, divine and human, or whether these two words are so different from each other that we cannot possibly treat them as if they were on the same level—not, so to speak, two subcategories of one general notion. In the short description of what the Bible is, at the beginning of this chapter, we saw that this "subject-object split" or this distinction between divine and human words can be found in the Bible. The Bible records God's "direct words," often introduced by the phrase, "Thus saith the Lord"; the Bible gives accounts of men's actions and reactions to God's actions and words; and finally, the Bible summarizes or records speeches or sermons made by men, for example, Peter's sermon in Acts 2. In spite of those differentiations we say that the Bible is "the Word of God." How far can we do this?

We can make this statement only when we see that God's Word occurs in different forms. There is only one reason for God's speaking to us, for our speaking to Him and for our preaching to others. That reason is Jesus Christ who is the Word Himself. But there is more than one form. We must distinguish between the forms of the Word and the reason for God's speaking. We have to be careful here. We are not at liberty to say that there are innumerable forms of the one Word of God— sermons, books, music, pictures, symbols, dreams, nature. This inclusiveness would go far beyond our question concerning the "Word." It would also deny the fact that God has chosen the Word as means of communication. It would bypass the fact that Christ is the Word made flesh. We are, therefore, not at liberty to name an endless series of "forms" of the Word of God. The prophetic and apostolic witness does not allow us to look for theoretical possibilities when we search for the forms of the Word of God. Since the Word of God does not grow out of our mind or our conception of God, we can understand the content as well as the form of the Word only when we look obediently to the historical concreteness of the Biblical witness. In this way we understand the forms of the witness by hearing the witness. Obedience to the witness enables us to understand that it is the one Word of God which is to be heard in three different forms. When we put all the emphasis on the hearing of the Word, then we are permitted to forget for a moment the possible dichotomy between the divine and human words, which will again be the subject of discussion later on. The self-disclosure of God in Christ has priority over our understanding of God and over our attempts to classify forms or categories in which God might reveal Himself. We must, therefore, begin to think about the Word and its forms not by abstract "thinking" concerning its theoretical possibilities, but by concrete listening to its factual forms. Admittedly, this statement implies truly a "theological" thought, i.e., a thought which does not begin with possibilities we can see but rather with facts which are proclaimed to us.[1] The beginning of "theological thinking" is, therefore, in a certain way illogical. We are absolutely unable to explain by way of proofs how we *begin* to think theologically or even what the result of such thinking will be. The thoughts of the Bible are in many ways contrary to the structure of thoughts of the "old man," or, more concretely, contrary to our thoughts which have been molded by Greek thinking and logic. This radical thought must be kept in mind constantly when we think about the practice of preaching.

When we take as the point of departure this obedient listening to the factual forms of the Word, then the Word presents itself *firstly* in its *proclaimed* form — in the actual proclamation, which has not only caused our interest in Christ, but also feeds us week after week in our life in the Church. Faith comes out of the sermon. (Romans 10:17.) There, in the sermon, it happens; we are confronted with the life-giving Word. If the sermon is really a sermon — the aim of this book is to clarify this point — then it is based on the Biblical witness to the life-giving Word that is Christ Himself. This *second* form in which the Word presents itself is the *written* form. Romans 10:17 says that faith comes out of the sermon, and it continues by saying that the sermon comes from the Word of God. The same thought is expressed in Acts 17:11, "For they received the word with all eagerness, examining the scriptures daily to see if these things were so." But the written form of the Word of God is not the ultimate form. The Bible is not the revelation. The Bible is the witness to the revelation of God in Christ. God's life-creating Word, with which He created the world and spoke to His servants, who later on gave witness to it in the books of the Old and New

[1] This is certainly seen differently by Paul Tillich in *Systematic Theology* Vol. I (Chicago: University of Chicago Press, 1951), pp. 8 ff., 106 ff., and Vol. II (Chicago: University of Chicago Press, 1957), pp. 13-16.

Testaments, can therefore be called the *revealed* form of the Word. As such it is the third form in which the Word presents itself. These are the "three forms of the Word of God." However, it must never be overlooked that these forms do not represent three words but are the three forms of the one Word of God.

It is not very important which terms are used to name these three forms. It was Karl Barth[2] who first elaborated them and gave them these names: (1) the proclaimed Word, (2) the written Word, (3) the revealed Word, and he numbered them in this order. It is God's one Word in three forms, one and the same God speaking, and one and the same Word spoken. Heinrich Vogel[3] preferred the opposite order, as did Otto Weber.[4] The latter speaks of: (1) the Word which has "happened," (2) the Word which is "witnessed," and (3) the Word which is "proclaimed." While it is not important how we name these forms of the Word, it is very important in which order we number them. It will be made clear below[5] why the order "proclaimed Word — written Word — revealed Word" is much more adequate than the opposite order.

There is an *analogy* between the three forms of the one Word and the three modes of being ("persons") of the one God. This is called the "Trinitarian analogy." There is obviously a relation between God the Father (the Creator) and the revealed Word, God the Son (the Reconciler) and the written Word, and God the Holy Spirit (the Redeemer) and the proclaimed Word. The New Testament seems to require these analogies. They are not artificial dogmatical constructions, but reflect truly the fact that it is the Father who creates and commands with His Word, that it is the Son who is the expectation of the Old and the witness of the New Testament, and that it is the Holy Spirit

[2] *Church Dogmatics*, Vol. I, Part I (New York: Charles Scribner's Sons, 1936), pp. 98-140.

[3] *Gott in Christo* (Berlin: Lettner Verlag, 1952), pp. 62 ff.; and *Christologie*, Vol. I (Munich: Chr. Kaiser Verlag, 1949), pp. 103 ff.

[4] *Grundlagen der Dogmatik*, Vol. I (Moers: Verlag Neukirchen, 1955), pp. 195 ff.

[5] See pp. 42 ff.

who leads us into the full truth after the Ascension. This is the
Biblical-theological reason that we can see an analogy between
the Father and the revealed Word, the Son and the Biblical
Word, and the Holy Spirit and the sermon. There are the three
modes of being ("persons") of God, but there is only one God;
and there are the three forms of the Word, but there is only
one Word.

However, the Bible can also say that the Holy Spirit, for
instance, spoke "by the mouth of David" (Acts 1:16), or that
Jesus is the Redeemer, or that the Spirit intercedes for us
(Romans 8:26), or that Jesus Christ is our "advocate" (1 John
2:1). There are also many "inconsistencies" to be found which
make it impossible for us to "describe" and comprehend God's
Word or the mystery of the Trinity in a logical or theological
"system," so as to enable us to explain everything in a mechanical
manner. In fact these passages, which deviate from the doctrine
of the Trinity or from this Trinitarian analogy, are not "illogical
exceptions," but in the Early Church they were the roots of the
doctrine of the *perichoresis*.[6] *Perichoresis* means that the three
persons of the Trinity cannot be separated as though they were
to be understood in isolation from each other. Over against this
thought we must think in terms of distinct "appropriations" in
order not to be completely negative in our thinking about the
Trinity. That is to say that the doctrine of the appropriations
was developed in the Early Church to balance the doctrine of
the *perichoresis*. It is a positive doctrine which aims at enabling
us to ascribe certain events in the divine work to certain persons
of the Trinity. For instance, it cannot be said that the Father
died on the cross (cf. the *patripassiani*); it was God the Son
who died for the sins of the world on the cross. Or, to use another
example, it cannot be said that Pentecost was the outpouring of
the Son; it was God the Holy Spirit who was poured out on the

---

[6] The word *perichoresis* means literally "flowing around" something, but
it is used to refer to the interpenetration of Father, Son, and Spirit. The
thought was elaborated by the Cappadocian Fathers, and by Hilary of
Poitiers (4th century).

Church and called it into being and enabled it to function. Each mode of being ("person") of the triune God has its *proprium*. This is what the doctrine of the appropriations means. But it is always important to keep in mind at the same time the *perichoresis* (or Augustine's *relationes*), which means that the *proprium* of a person of the Trinity is not one-third of the triune God, as if God could be separated into three parts.

Having been elaborated in the Early Church, these doctrines were expressed by the Early Church in the creeds, which were accepted by the Churches of the Reformation. Although they are unknown to many of our church members, these doctrines are an extremely important basis for any constructive theological thinking. By joining the Church our church members consciously or unconsciously accept these doctrines because they are included in the work of preparation and elaboration of the great creeds which are accepted by most of the major denominations. If we accept these doctrines as a true interpretation of the prophetic and apostolic witness of the Bible, and if we further accept the so-called "Trinitarian analogy," then we can reach some basic conclusions with regard to the question of preaching. The precise statement is this: God the Father is graciously acting in Jesus Christ, who is witnessed to by the books of the Bible; He acts again and again in His mercy in the Holy Spirit by leading His children into the truth, by enabling them to witness to Him, and by making it possible for them to pray (worship). We will primarily be interested in the last part of this thought: that God (the Father in Jesus Christ) is acting in the Holy Spirit when two or three are gathered together in His name, that is, when the assembly of the saints is worshiping on Sunday. We have already agreed — and everyone will agree here — that the Biblical witness must be understood in "relation" to Jesus Christ. In the same way and with the same certainty it can now be said that the life of the Church must be understood in "relation" to the Holy Spirit. Preaching, as an important part of the life of the Church, can therefore be called a *proprium* of the Holy Spirit. The sermon is the expression of the movement from the written form of the Word of God to the proclaimed form of the Word. Strictly speaking, the sermon, as it is preached from the pulpit, is the end of this movement. It is in itself the proclaimed form of the Word of God. The same thought can be expressed in terms which have been used above: there is only one Word of the one God; it presents itself in three forms. The task of the preacher is to study the second form of the Word of God (the written form) in order to hear and to understand how this written form can break through to its first form (the proclaimed form). If the "Trinitarian analogy" is true, then we can say that it is God himself who acts through the Holy Spirit in Christ, who wants to make Himself known by the preaching of the sermon. Hence, it is impossible to say that a sermon is merely a description of what God is or does, or a repetition of what He was or has done, or a meditation on what He shall be or do. Nor can a sermon be a reflection, an evaluation, a memorial, an instruction, or a mere repetition of the words of the Bible. God wants the sermon to be His own living voice. There is only one Word of God. Therefore, it must be considered to be unbiblical to assume that a true sermon is of less power than the sayings of Jeremiah or the words of the Sermon on the Mount or an Epistle of Paul.

These thoughts about the three forms of the Word of God and the "Trinitarian analogy" lead to the first fundamental statement about preaching: the content or essence, the principle or point of departure, the guiding thought or criterion of our work when preparing a sermon is not a theological thought or an aspect of the Biblical message, e.g., the love of God, the grace of God, the Kingdom of God, the office of reconciliation, the salvation or conversion of men, etc. It is all this, but it is primarily and above all the free and merciful decision of the will of the triune God to work in Jesus Christ through the Holy Spirit with the preacher and his people, in such a way that the miracle happens that the second form of the Word (the written Bible) breaks through into the first form (the proclamation). Then it is that the word of the sermon truly becomes the one

Word of the one God in this very form of proclamation. This thought can be expressed in simpler language by saying that Jesus Christ is the Word of God which is witnessed to us in the Bible; that it is the preacher's task to preach the good news of the Bible; and that he will be enabled by the Holy Spirit to do this, so that God's voice is really being heard on Sunday. All this is correct language, but we must know what we mean when we use this language.

2. THE AUTHORITY OF THE WORD

Jesus Christ is the Preacher who proclaims Himself. It is His will to make Himself known. He places the preacher in the service of His Word. The authority of the preaching man is not a derivation or reflection, not an experience or a "status"; it is the gift of the presence of Jesus Christ in the Holy Spirit. This given authority is not smaller or less important than Christ's authority, for He is the Preacher Himself.

When preaching is understood as the proclaimed Word of God, which is based on the written form of the Word, everything turns upon the fact that the Word is truly God's Word and therefore His action. The way must be free for Him to use "my mouth" so that He speaks. Infinite obedience would be necessary for this. But the only obedient human being is the human man Jesus Christ. So He is the only real Preacher, as much as He is the real High Priest, King, and Prophet. He is the Preacher *kat' exochen*, who proclaims Himself. He is His own Evangelist. If any other human beings attempt to do — or are commanded to do! — a work which can only be done on grounds of this perfect obedience of Jesus Christ, they can only do it "in Christ." The task of proclamation is given to the whole Church, and the Church can only fulfill this task because it is formed into one body with Christ by the Holy Spirit. The

Church participates in the ministry of Christ.[7] It is only in this participation that the work of the Church can be done, and this participation is the only reason that the Word of the sermon has authority.

It would not really be helpful to talk about a "derived" authority, as if our human words were only in a certain way words of authority, or as if only some of our words were "the real Word of God," while all the others were only human expressions of human opinions which do not really matter. This approach would lead to an unfortunate dichotomy between "real" and "unreal" words of our human witness. It would ultimately mean that only the Biblical quotations in our sermons were the true and authentic proclamation while all the rest would only serve to link up one quotation with the other. Obviously, this approach does not make sense, especially since the very same skepticism could be applied to the Bible, which also represents words spoken by man to God as well as words spoken by God to men. The division between divine and human words in a sermon would necessarily lead to the same division in the Bible. We would then actually have two Bibles in one volume: a collection of divine Biblical words and another collection of human Biblical words. Where could we draw the line between the two? How could we single out the "divine" words and separate them from the mere historical reports or the words and prayers of the patriarchs, prophets, and apostles? We are not only unable to do this, but it is also clear that the whole attempt to do so would indicate a completely wrong understanding of the Biblical witness. We must remember, however, that the Biblical theology of the last century proceeded in exactly this fashion. By the beginning of this century it was the generally accepted opinion that "the words of our Lord" are more important than other parts of the Bible. In our churches many ministers and Sunday school teachers still think and teach that the Sermon on the

[7] Elaborated by T. F. Torrance, *Royal Priesthood* (Edinburgh: Oliver & Boyd, 1955) (*Scottish Journal of Theology* Occasional Papers No. 3), Chapter II, especially pp. 35-38.

Mount is more "valuable" than a chapter in one of the Epistles, or that a "word of the Lord" is more authoritative than a word spoken by a prophet or an apostle. They are often not aware of the dangerous results which might flow out of this conception: that the Bible is divided into two parts, an authoritative divine part and a less important historical part. These people are therefore afraid of Biblical criticism, because they quite rightly recognize that Biblical criticism can seriously damage and even destroy their whole conception of the Bible. Hence they defend each "word of the Lord" as a genuine and authentic saying and only very seldom will they admit that a "word of Jesus" was not spoken by Jesus Himself but written by the early witnesses. Here we have the whole dilemma of Biblical theology![8]

It follows logically that Biblical "conservatism," the attitude of "defending" as many genuine words of Jesus as possible (thereby devaluating other parts of the Bible), must necessarily be "liberalism" when it comes to the question of preaching. This can easily be proved by experience in the Church. As soon as one separates or distinguishes "divine" and "human" words in the Bible, or "words of Jesus" and other words, one is bound to say that our (human) sermons in the Church cannot be the Word of God. Only quotations from the Bible — but only from the "divine" parts of the Bible! — can then be the authoritative parts of our sermons. All the rest is nothing other than repetition, amplification, application, interpretation or in one word "teaching." Such an unfortunate confusion is only possible if one does not accept the understanding of the three forms of the Word of God.

If one leaves out the doctrine of the three forms of the Word of God, the following false conceptions of the authority of the Word spoken in our worship services are the only alternatives:

a. The understanding that Scripture — or part of Scripture — is "objective," while all our own words are subjective. The whole

[8] James M. Robinson, *A New Quest of the Historical Jesus* (London: SCM Press, 1959), describes the recent history of this problem and tries to work toward a solution.

worship service is divided into two parts. Only Scripture reading is objective. The liturgical movements will tend to this conception and will ultimately reach the point that the sacraments are conceived to be the most objective part of our worship, because here even the words of the Bible, and above all the words of the Lord (or even the Lord Himself!) have become external objects. The Mass without a sermon is the caricature of this misconception of the division between subject and object. The Mass guarantees the presence of Christ and enables the worshipers to participate objectively in the givenness of forgiveness.

b. The understanding that the ordination of the minister guarantees the objectivity and validity of the spoken Word. He has been given the special grace or special gift of being God's very own messenger whose words are hallowed by the (sacrament of) ordination to this holy office. He has been "set apart" and his words are therefore more authentic and of a higher degree of authority than the words of other members of the Church. Only ordained men can preach the Word and pronounce the benediction; laymen cannot preach but only teach. A variation of this conception would be the idea that the consecrated church building and especially the altar with the elements of communion guarantee the objectivity and validity of the words which are spoken or read during a worship service.

c. The understanding that the "indwelling Spirit" enables a man to preach objectively the Word and Will of God. Regeneration makes it possible for believers to go beyond their own subjectivity; having the "new life," they become tools of the Holy Spirit and speak out directly what God wants to say to His people. Any man can have this gift; ordination is the formal confirmation or recognition of a man's regeneration, which can be noticed by all the other believers because of the confession the candidate has made, and because of the holy life he lives. The Bible is only a source book, whereas what is really important is the personal conversion and the conviction that the Holy

Spirit renews our lives. The sermon will therefore primarily be a confession of one's own experience.

These three types of misconception of the living Word are symbolized by the labels "sacramentalism," "Roman Catholicism," and "theologia regenitorum" or spiritualism of the sects. It is evident that they are not mutually exclusive but in practice are so closely connected with one another that often they can hardly be distinguished. And it is also evident that all three of them contain a factor which under certain circumstances cannot be totally denied. The difficulty is that they do violence to the Biblical Word and promise, in spite of the fact that they appear to be "conservative." They are in fact "liberal" — to use terms of the theology of the last century — because they do not dare to see and to accept that God in His freedom has chosen human witnesses in all their subjectivity to preach His living Word, which is both subject and object of our sermon. This must now be explained.

We have seen that the doctrine of the three forms of the Word of God and the "Trinitarian analogy" enable us to understand the relation between the revealed, the written, and the spoken Word. We may think of the proclamation in the Church in terms of ecclesiology, which cannot be separated from pneumatology, because the life in the Church is the work *(proprium)* of the Holy Spirit. The saving and judging Word which is spoken by and in the Church receives its authority from the written Word, which we understand in terms of Christology. Or, in other words, our understanding of the "divine and human parts" in the Bible cannot possibly be separated from Jesus Christ who is witnessed to by the books of the Bible. It is Jesus Christ as true man and true God, *vere homo et vere deus,* who is witnessed to by the Bible. This is the so-called "Christological analogy." That is: if it is true that the witness of the Bible is, according to the gracious will of the triune God, witness toward Jesus Christ (in the Old Testament) and witness from Jesus Christ (in the New Testament), it must follow that Scripture also shares the humiliation and the form of the servant of the Lord, and not just his glorification. The humiliated (the "low") Jesus of Nazareth in His full humanity must be seen in relation to the full humanity of the Biblical witnesses, and the exalted (the "high") Jesus Christ in His full deity must be seen in relation to the full deity of the Biblical witnesses. And it is the one and the same Jesus Christ, true God and true man, who is witnessed to in the books of the Bible. A philosophical distinction between divine and human words is no longer possible, for Jesus Christ is God's Word to us and He is also in our (human) place when we speak to God in our prayers and when we preach to men in our sermons. This is true for the Biblical witnesses, and it is also true for us.

It is important not to lose sight of this analogy between the "natures" of Christ and the Bible. Aside from this analogy, there are basically two alternatives. There is the fundamentalist conception of the Bible, which betrays a docetic Christology; or there is a merely historical approach to the Bible, which betrays an Ebionitic Christology. When it comes to preaching, the two heresies present themselves in the following ways:

a. The idea that the Biblical Word is so divine and heavenly that it is actually "un-human" will lead us to the error that a sermon is merely an effort to convey and make known divine truths in human words, in such a way that it is taken for granted that those timeless truths can never really find their way to the low level of everyday, human existence unless a spiritual miracle should happen. We will, therefore, try desperately to "get the message across," to "make it relevant," to "communicate," because we do not trust the Word of God in its very humanness[9] and worldliness to make itself relevant. This is indeed the docetic heresy.

        [9] The term "humanness" is to be preferred to "humanity" in order better to present the contrast with "worldliness"; "humanity" is often associated with "humanitarian."

b. The opposite view, the merely historical approach to the Bible, leads us to the error that the sermon is an attempt to lift people up from the low level of their existence to a higher level of "spiritual life," or even to the height of God. We will appeal to people's emotions and religiosity in order to cultivate their "spiritual experiences." In our sermons we will refer to "great Christians" or to "saints" in the history of the Church, in order to stimulate our people's desire to make a new effort to imitate those "spiritual leaders" of the Church. We will even create the desire in our people's hearts to have a "great preacher" in their pulpit; and we ourselves will appreciate being recognized as one of them. This indeed is the Ebionitic heresy.

It is amazing to see how often these two conceptions of preaching are practiced by one and the same preacher or author in the homiletical field. The roots of the two definitions are opposed to each other, but the practical conclusions drawn out of them are very similar. In both cases the sermon is conceived as work of man, and faith is synergistically understood as an effort of man. Either of these errors will not escape a type of ecclesiology that is an end in itself: the word which comes *to* the Church, actually comes *from* the Church. The Church is in conversation with herself; the sermon says what the Church already believes. The faith of the Church is being preached; the sermon repeats only what the people already know and like to hear. This would even be less helpful than Schleiermacher's conception of proclamation, which is based on the self-consciousness of the Church's faith. It is quite clear that those approaches which attempt to comprehend the authority of the proclaimed Word by leaving out the Christological understanding of authority are necessarily spiritualistic, miraculous, or moralistic. The Word becomes static and dead; it is only a Word of the past and not a Word for today. Hence the sermon must be understood idealistically, and it will deal with ideas and principles, which can be elaborated, expounded and taught by homiletical textbooks.[10] No longer is Jesus Christ the Preacher who proclaims Himself through the mouth of His ignorant and sinful servants; but the clergyman becomes the preacher who must strive to a maximum of faith, sinlessness, Christian example, and eloquence as the necessary prerequisities for an authoritative preacher.[11]

The authority of the Biblical Word, as well as of the proclaimed Word, cannot be separated from Jesus Christ, and this means concretely — from His presence. Christ is not the authority "behind" the words of His witnesses; rather He is in their words in His very presence. In His absence, the words would not have authority, even if they were "orthodox" words or Bible verses. The presence of Christ, however, does not automatically mean that His power and Lordship are directly and unmistakenly revealed, as if each sermon should *"ex opere operato"* convert all people present. This assumption would also indicate a docetic Christology or at least a philosophical conception of revelation. If the hiddenness of Jesus Christ is not taken seriously it is either because the manhood of Jesus Christ is overlooked or because the eschatological fulfillment has been impatiently projected into our time, which is still the time in which the Church shares the humiliation and the sufferings of Christ.

The "Christological analogy" has been found necessary to understand the authority of Scripture. Since the proclaimed Word, the sermon, cannot be separated from the written Word, the Scripture, the Christological analogy also throws light on our understanding of the authority of the sermon. The "humanness" of the Bible as well as of our sermons must be understood

[10] Cf. an advertisement for a book in the *British Weekly*, September 4, 1958: "Preaching—the Art of Communication. Every preacher, if he is to be successful, has to master the art of 'getting over.' Writing from many years of experience as a preacher, _____ makes a frankly psychological approach to the nature of preaching, the personality of the preacher, and his relationship with the congregation."

[11] Even with the greatest amount of good will, it cannot be seen why this attitude is different from the techniques of political party ideologies (East and West) and other great religions in our world!

in relation to the manhood and humiliation of Jesus Christ. The death and the glorification of Christ are not the "objects" or topics of our sermons, but we always carry "in the body the death of Jesus, so that the life of Jesus may be manifested in our bodies. For while we live we are always being given up to death for Jesus' sake, so that the life of Jesus may also be manifested in our mortal flesh." (2 Corinthians 4:10-11.) We must acknowledge the mystery of the person of Jesus Christ if we want to know who and where we are when we preach, "for what we preach is not ourselves, but Jesus Christ as Lord." (2 Corinthians 4:5.)

The Christological as well as the Trinitarian analogy is indeed — as are all analogies in theology[12] — a daring undertaking. It is not by accident that Karl Barth is careful not to use these analogies to the extreme. The difficult question now confronts us as to how else we would proceed if we wanted to avoid the employment of theological analogies, which are clearly used by some of the Biblical writers. It is comparatively easy to argue against analogy, and this becomes almost a fashion today, but it is difficult to provide a substitute for it. We have already seen that in the case of the question of the authority of the Word the attempts to proceed without the analogy to the two "natures" of Christ lead us to alternatives which are not really acceptable. James Barr of Edinburgh has written an interesting critique[13] of J. K. S. Reid's book, *The Authority of Scripture*,[14] where Dr. Reid uses the Christological analogy in much the same way that Karl Barth did. Barr says that this analogy could falsely lead to a splitting of a human and a divine element, so that the human element would be considered to be a word without authority, while it is just this human word which is the word of authority. God is calling His people in such a way that their

[12] Cf. the critical article by John McIntyre, "Analogy," *Scottish Journal of Theology*, Vol. XII, No. 1, March 1959.
[13] *Scottish Journal of Theology*, Vol. II, No. 1, March 1958.
[14] Published in U.S.A. by Harper & Brothers, 1957.

(human!) words (tradition) are really words of authority.[15] "God elects into existence His People, He elects into existence their tradition."[16] The words that matter are words spoken by God's people. Authority is made manifest in election. It is interesting to see that the critique of the analogy comes from the area of Old Testament discipline, and that it does not represent the fear that the "divine" element in Scripture might be underestimated, but just the opposite — that the neglect of the words of man *to* God in the books of the Bible would dissolve all authority of the Bible. It can be questioned, however, whether the analogy with the two natures of Christ will really lead to a splitting of two "elements" in the Bible, so that we had to fear for one or the other. This splitting is just what should not happen according to Chalcedon. In any case, it is fruitful to find in Barr's article an attempt to think of the third form of the Word (the revealed Word) without being driven to G. Ernest Wright's reduction of God's words to actions. Wright indeed reduces God's words in the Old Testament to "mere" actions by understanding the Biblical words as interpretations of God's actions with His people.[17] According to his approach it should be possible to say that God has never spoken, i.e., that there never was a "third form of the Word," but that He "spoke" by action. It depends, of course, on a clarification of the dogmatical meaning of these terms whether we can go along with this approach or not. But it seems to be inevitable that Wright has to begin with an analysis of the historical facts in the history of Israel, so much so that the words which were written later, namely the Biblical witness, can only be considered after the historical events have been examined, in which archaeological evidence plays a major role. This can be avoided only if we keep in mind the order in which the three forms of the Word are placed.[18]

[15] "Tradition and Expectation in Ancient Israel," *Scottish Journal of Theology*, Vol. X, No. 1, March 1957.

[16] Barr, *Scottish Journal of Theology*, March 1958, p. 91.

[17] Cf. *God Who Acts, Biblical Theology as Recital* (Chicago: Henry Regnery Company, 1952).

[18] Cf. p. 29.

We have seen that it is indeed the "revealed Word" which gives authority to the written Word, and that it is the written Word (the Bible) which gives authority to the proclaimed Word. This is the order: 3-2-1, the order of authority. But this is not the order in which we *hear* the Word. To exaggerate for clarification: we do not first dig in the sand and try to find archaeological and historical evidence, then go to the Bible to prove that the Bible is right, and then move to the Church in our generation to proclaim that since such and such happened, and since it was interpreted in the Bible in this and that way, it will also be true today, if we only recognize and interpret it rightly. This is the order of authority, and, for that matter, the order of succession of historical events in God's history with his people.[19] But this is not the order in which we see and hear when we are confronted with the living Word, i.e., with Christ Himself who is present when two or three are gathered in His name. We hear and understand in the order 1-2-3: proclaimed, written, revealed Word. If we follow Otto Weber and Heinrich Vogel's opposite order, we might rightly be asked by Wright what and how we know anything at all about this "revealed" Word which God has spoken? Then we must use his own answer: we know the Word by historical and archaeological analysis of historical events. Over against this, the Biblical witness says that faith comes from the sermon, that we are confronted with the life-giving Word through the testimony of another brother, and that only then can we go back to the Scriptures. "For they received the word with all eagerness, examining the scriptures daily to see if these things were so." (Acts 17:11.) The proper order is the searching "backwards" (from the Word which gave life to me when I heard it) to the Scriptures, in order to hear the "revealed" Word. This order is true in the same way that it is true that we cannot say anything about the Son — namely "Jesus is Lord" — except by the "Holy Spirit." (1 Corinthians 12:3.) It is not the

[19] It can also be the order of teaching, and it is apparently in this sense that Otto Weber and Heinrich Vogel want to be understood.

Son who teaches us who the Holy Spirit is, but the other way
around. And it is not the Father who teaches us who the Son is,
but the Son leads us to the Father, and there is no other way
to Him. And yet, the Church teaches the *processio spiritus ex
patre filioque:* the Spirit proceeds from the Father and the Son.
The intention of this formulation was never that we should first
investigate who the Father is, then who the Son is, in order
finally to understand who the Spirit is. We see here that the
"Trinitarian analogy" is inevitable and very helpful: it is not
used as a proof, but rather as an aid for the proper understanding of what God has provided in the revelation of His Son. The
order of authority of the Word is 3-2-1, but the order in which
we are confronted with the Word is 1-2-3. Karl Barth chose this
order deliberately to make it unmistakably clear; it was elaborated by him long before Old Testament scholars, represented
by W. F. Albright and G. Ernest Wright, had begun to raise the
question of the "forms of the Word" as an indirect result of
their archeological studies. It must be seen, however, that their
method is only rejected here in the context of our consideration of
preaching; how far the approach of these scholars has its own
right in the field of historical research is quite a different question. It should be maintained that for our understanding of the
authority and practice of preaching we must not confuse the
order of the forms of the Word; or by way of analogy, we are
not able to understand the first article of the Apostolic Creed
until we have heard the second and third ones. Therefore,
preaching is the first form of the Word (the *proprium* of the
Holy Spirit), and not the third. If we said the third were the
first, we would have a preconception of what "the Word" should
be before we have heard it.[20]

No one can debate away the logical contradiction that the

[20] We will have to come back to this question of the order when we ask
how teaching differs from preaching. (See p. 103.) We will see that it is
possible and perhaps necessary to proceed in the order 3-2-1 when we
teach, but that we can only teach after we have been confronted with the
Word in the order 1-2-3.

sermon is the Word *of* the Church and at the same time the Word *to* the Church. This is the logical difficulty which we have concerning the mystery of the person of Jesus Christ: true God and true man, not successively, but simultaneously. If we separate the understanding of the words spoken and heard in the Church from this basic point of departure for all our theological thinking, we will end up in a hopeless dilemma.

The following conclusion, which will be the basis for our thinking about preaching, can now be formulated:

God is known because He makes Himself known. The Word with which God reveals Himself appears in three forms. We understand these forms in analogy to the Trinity. We see also an analogy of the Servanthood and Lordship of Christ to the humanness and glory of the Bible, on the one hand, and to the humanness and glory of the sermon, on the other hand. God's words and acts cannot be separated; it is God who acts when His Word is preached. The sermon is an act of God the Father in Jesus Christ through the Holy Spirit. The sermon, therefore, cannot be mere exegesis, reflection, meditation, repetition, or "theology made simple" in the form of preaching. The sermon must be understood as an acting of the risen Lord through the Holy Spirit in the "Communion of the Saints." Because Jesus Christ Himself is the Preacher, the second form of the Word — the written Bible — "yearns" to become a sermon (the first form). The word of a preaching man can only be a word which serves this one Word of God that wants to break through from its second to its first form. For it is God's will to make Himself known, and it is His call that places His children in the service of His Word; they are *Verbi divini ministri*, or "ministers" as it is expressed in English. The authority of the preaching man is not a derivation or reflection, not an experience or a "status"; it is the gift of the presence of Jesus Christ. This given authority, then, is not smaller or less important than Christ's authority, for He is the Preacher Himself. The presence of Christ in the Holy Spirit, in His own authority, necessitates the following statements:

a. The act of proclaiming the Word of God is a service to the act which is performed by Jesus Christ Himself. This makes it impossible to say that only the minister or specially consecrated people "share" this service and the righteousness and obedience of Christ. The whole Church receives this gift. Therefore the whole Church shares the responsibility for the proclamation.

b. It is not possible to value "liturgy" higher than preaching. Scripture readings, which are a repetition of the second form of the Word of God, cannot be more valuable, correct, true, divine, etc., than preaching. The Scripture passages "want" to be preached. The Bible has, so to speak, the "self will" to break through to proclamation.

c. It is one and the same human word, the word with which we lie, boast, or offend and hurt others, which is used by God in the service of proclaiming His humiliation and glorification in Christ. (Cf. James 3:9-10.) It is true that we cannot speak about God with our human words, but it is equally true that God uses just these words to make Himself known. It is God who acts when the Word is proclaimed.

All this is summarized in the statement that preaching on the grounds of the Biblical witness is *self-proclamation by Jesus Christ*. Human witness is participation in this action of Jesus Christ. It is, strictly speaking, participation in revelation! Christ or His words and acts are not the "topics" of our sermons, but we are the "topic" of the wisdom and thoughts of God's action in Christ. This was not only the case in the "time of the Bible," lest we adore a God who is dead and conduct services which are memorial feasts of His former actions! We must first see and say that the Word, Jesus Christ, is the subject of the preaching function; only then can we say that the Word is the object of preaching.

3. THE WORLDLINESS OF THE WORD

The "Christological analogy" should not lead to a static system. There are no "Christian principles," for God's call and man's response are both grounded in the obedience of Jesus Christ, who is God's Word to us. Because it is the living Christ who gives the call and the response, our response is concrete and immediate, not indirect or derived. The Word of God is not a religious but a worldly word that comes to our world in the incarnate Christ, who makes Himself relevant to those whom He calls to respond.

There is a certain danger in making a "system" of the Christological analogy, which was found to be so helpful for the understanding of the authority of the word of the witness. A scholastic approach to the "doctrine of the two natures" has always led to an understanding of Jesus Christ in static terms; and, indeed, the word "nature" itself points to a static and dead Christ. The result of such thinking can be a philosophical ontology which depersonalizes the event of Jesus Christ and turns it into a timeless fact, truth, or statement. Exactly the same thing can happen if we use analogy to apply a Christological ontology to the question of the Word of the Bible and the word of the pulpit. It is difficult to avoid ontological thinking, for we want to maintain under all circumstances that the Christ event and the Gospel, which gives witness to it, are indeed true, valid, and factual, whether we happen to believe them or not. The easiest way to avoid ontological theologizing would be to turn to an existentialist conception, which would ultimately mean that the Gospel would be true only if we believed it. This is just what we do not want to say. However, it should be quite clear that the criticism of existentialism should not imply that we overlook the immense importance of the Word "at the moment," or in other words: the unique significance of the hour here and now, when I am met by Jesus Christ, and when I am called upon to respond.

For our understanding of the proclamation of the life-giving Word, everything depends upon the fact that the action of God in Jesus Christ with His people is, so to speak, "in motion." God speaks, we hear, and it is up to us to act. He calls and we respond. This happens time and again. It is not once and for all that God speaks and we respond. And it is not merely that God repeats His Word again and again, so that we respond in the same way again and again, but that even the content of God's Word is different yesterday, today, and tomorrow. For this reason it is impossible to speak of "Christian principles," i.e., "timeless truths." How then are we to know what our response should be, if it cannot be derived from principles? Our response can only be obedient because of the obedience of Jesus Christ. We say that He is in perfect union with the Father, and by this we mean that He is perfectly obedient; "the Son can do nothing of his own accord, but only what he sees the Father doing; for whatever he does, the Son does likewise." (John 5:19.) It is not out of a miraculous and systematic knowledge that Jesus Christ is obedient to the Father. He was not "obedient unto death, even death on a cross" (Philippians 2:8), as though He had systematized His thoughts and had said to Himself that He would be raised after three days and would be highly exalted and would receive a name above every name. Likewise, our obedience cannot be grounded in a system or refer back to theological conceptions or to an exegesis which we, or another person, have made some time ago. The response to what God says now is immediate response. To trust in His Word is to trust in the Word I hear now, not in the Word I remember, or in the Word I might expect. It is the immediate and concrete obedience of Jesus Christ that enables us to respond obediently. It is in His name that we are gathered to hear the Word, and it is in His name that we respond to it and are on our way to preach it. We can only say this because of the humanity of the Lord, and it is highly important that the Church has long confessed that the manhood of Christ did not cease to exist after the Ascension. For this very reason we can and must speak about the humanity or manhood of the risen Lord. In naive but rather plain language, we can say that we hear with the ears of Christ and also respond with the obedience of Christ.

It is almost unnecessary to say that this participation in the obedience of Christ does not mean that Christians "become" Christ. To follow Christ and to share His righteousness and obedience cannot be confused with the uniqueness of the Son of God, whose actions are His deeds, and whose deeds are His actions. Jesus Christ is elected and appointed as the Messiah; this can by no means be said of Christians. They are not elected to be Christs, but they are elected "in him" to the sonship "through Jesus Christ" (Ephesians 1:4, 5), so that they are real and true men who can live in righteousness and obedience before God. Confusion between Christ and the Christian would also indicate that we did not realize the preliminary character of the life in the Church, which still waits for fulfillment. But Christ Jesus takes us into His obedience; He takes us into His prayer. We can take part in His work "for we are fellow workmen for God." (1 Corinthians 3:9.)

In other words, the analogy of the "natures" of Christ must be seen in terms of functions, not in terms of different types of an ontological status. Thus the Word of God and the word of His witnesses are not derived from principles or ideas. "Christian principles" do not exist, and in our preaching and teaching we should not even use this expression, lest we open the door to serious misunderstandings. Nor is the Word of God and the word of His witnesses a "religious word."[21] The life-giving and judging Word comes to us in the worldliness of our world. To make it a "religious" word is to remove it from the life and the world in which we live. The Word became flesh and it is where we are. The holy Word of God is so much with and among us that we can even despise it, or use it for false purposes, or quote and

[21] Cf. the helpful clarifications of these thoughts and terms in Alan Richardson, *An Introduction to the Theology of the New Testament* (New York: Harper & Brothers, 1958), pp. 377 ff: "The NT writers, however, do not think of the Christian 'way' as 'religion' at all."

exegete it against the will of the living God; and all this can be done without being punished in a way that could be seen or proved. This is what must be called the "insecurity of the Word,"[22] or the "servant form" of the Word.[23] It is God's will to reveal Himself in a dialogue with His people in worldly words, and it is His will that they give answer and response in worldly words and not in heavenly language.[24] The desperation concerning "communication" in homiletical literature and in discussions among preachers indicates very clearly that the Word of God is wrongly conceived as a religious Word, which one has to "make" relevant, as if it were not the Word itself that makes itself relevant. Thus Paul M. van Buren writes, in an excellent article on preaching, "God's Word is life itself. For a world that lies in death, the Word is the resurrection and the life. There can be no question of our making the Word relevant to the world. The Word has already made itself relevant to the world: He did so when He created this world and reconciled it to Himself!"[25] Or even more clearly: "It is absurd for us to worry as we do about 'making the Bible relevant.' The Word of God is far more relevant than we could ever be, and if we will be obedient to the Bible, truly obedient, then we shall find ourselves far more deeply involved in the lives of our people and in the 'situation' than we ever were when we were anxious to be 'relevant.' God's Word is devastatingly relevant when it is truly preached and truly heard."[26] Jesus Christ is God's Word here on earth; He did not establish a higher platform in this world to meet His people, but He went to the lowest regions. (Ephesians 4:9.) In the course of the history of the Church, this aspect

[22] Otto Weber, *Grundlagen der Dogmatik,* Vol. I, p. 198.

[23] Vogel, *Gott in Christo,* pp. 101 ff.

[24] An exception is the *"glossolalia,"* the speaking in tongues, but 1 Corinthians 14 makes it quite clear that those words are to be interpreted in normal language, lest they serve an egotistical desire for a connection between an individual and God and thus not edify the Church.

[25] "The Word of God in the Church," *Anglican Theological Review,* October 1957, p. 348.

[26] *Ibid.,* p. 354.

has long been overlooked due to the influence of the hellenistic mystery religions. The neglect of the seriousness of the Incarnation is expressed only too clearly in the church architecture of the Middle Ages, which tried to create an otherworldy atmosphere for the worshipers who were, for the period of worship, separated from their daily work, homes, and fellow men. Although it restricts and even denies the fullness of the Incarnation, this theology is supported by us if we deliberately sympathize with that church architecture and in addition call the church building a "sanctuary," which is properly a name for God's people, never for a building. (1 Corinthians 3:16-17; 6:19; 2 Corinthians 6:16; Hebrews 9:11-12.)

Instead of speaking about the "worldliness of the Word," we could also use the expression "secular" and consequently speak of the "secular Word," which is by God's decision the form in which He makes Himself known. It is indeed the language of our *"saeculum"* in which the Good News must be preached; it cannot be a special church language (for instance Latin) that should be preferred to our normal means of communication. If we say, however, that the Word of God is and must be a "secular Word," we must distinguish this Word very sharply from "profane words." I am met by Jesus Christ in worldly and secular words, and I must respond to Him in those words; but His words are by no means profane words, nor can the words of my response and of my sermon be profane! We touch here the fundamental difference indicated by the Biblical expressions "in the world" and "of the world," or, in Pauline language, "in the flesh" and "of the flesh." Profanity has its roots and takes its content "from the world" and from the flesh. Not so the Word of the living God. His Word comes indeed "from Him," but it comes to me, and that means that it comes "in the flesh" and "into the world." If we do not carefully keep this distinction in mind, either we will turn the Gospel into complete profanity, i.e., we will make a philosophical, ethical, or moral system out of it, or we will turn it into a religion, i.e., something that is constantly "above" our heads and can only be expressed in idealistic terms.

In D. T. Niles we have one of the clearest voices among English-speaking theologians teaching us that the Gospel of Christ is not a religion.[27] When he explains what "religion-less Christianity" is,[28] we hear in different words addressed to a different audience exactly what Dietrich Bonhoeffer expressed so profoundly in his letters and papers from prison.[29] There should be no preacher in our generation who carelessly bypasses these books.

Although the world tries to redeem itself and to get rid of its own sins and shortcomings, the world that does not know the offer and claim of Jesus Christ is a highly religious world. Only ignorance of the New Testament language can suggest to us that the word "world" describes a "secular" realm of existence. In Biblical times there was no "secularized" world, and it is really questionable now whether such a world exists. It is precisely a world that is pregnant with religions, i.e., loaded with attempts at self-justification, and self-redemption, that is addressed in the New Testament and that must hear the justifying and redeeming Word of God in Christ. This is the world the disciples will fear according to the words of their Master. (John 16:33.) But they will not try to escape from it, because Jesus Christ loves it, came into it, and died for it. Its power is broken and new life is offered to it. The religions of the world try to teach people how to reach another, better world — preferably with the help of a god who belongs to another or an "upper" world. Jesus Christ, however, is the Word made flesh, who meets us right at the roots of these thoughts and activities and converts us and sends us into the world.

We are accustomed to the thought that the world in itself is evil and sinful. The statement has been made so often that we take it as the presupposition of the Gospel, so much so that we

---

[27] *The Preacher's Task and the Stone of Stumbling* (New York: Harper & Brothers, 1958), pp. 61-68, 70-77, 97, *et al.* Also *Preaching the Gospel of the Resurrection* (Philadelphia: The Westminster Press, 1953).

[28] *Preacher's Task,* p. 68.

[29] *Prisoner for God,* pp. 121-125.

very often believe (and practice!) that we should preach the "sinfulness" of the world before preaching forgiveness, or — in the language of the preacher — that we should tell the people that there is "a need for God." There is no need for God that we could describe psychologically or rhetorically; people can be quite happy without knowing God. Prior to the Enlightenment the world view implied for all people the idea that God had to be taken into account in their thinking about the world and man. In that sense one could say that they experienced a "need for God." At the latest after the industrial revolution, the world was thought of as independent of and self-sufficient apart from God. In this sense there is no subjective "need for God."[30]

The Biblical statement that there is indeed sin, darkness, and damnation is used first of all with regard to Israel, God's very own people! They become the enemies of God and they are in sin. This situation can only be seen after God has spoken; it cannot be used as a "preparation" in order to preach His Word more effectually. We read in the Prologue to John's Gospel that the light came into the darkness and that God's own people did not receive it. And so we must understand it: evil is the world, dark is the situation, and lost are the people when the Word of the living God is not accepted — even though the world was created good. (Genesis 1:31.) The world "as such" is not evil or good or something in between. To say anything like that is a speculation which does not help us, but only confuses us; especially if we attempt to use those thoughts to improve the technique or effectiveness of our sermons.

The greatest confusion would be the conception (which has

[30] I cannot see why it should necessarily be true that man should be driven "to the quest for revelation" on the grounds of his existential questions, as Tillich says. (*Systematic Theology*, Vol. I, pp. 71-105, especially 94 and 100; cf. also the Introduction to Vol. II.) Nor can I understand on the basis of the Biblical texts that man must experience a "shaking of the foundations" before he can receive the "answer" of revelation (e.g., Vol. I, pp. 62 and 110). "Only those who have . . . totally questioned the meaning of existence can understand what the symbol of the Kingdom of God means" (p. 62).

often been held in the history of the Church) that there are
two powers or two gods, a good god and an evil god, or an
upper world which is good, and a lower world which is evil,
and that one should tell people that they are to trust the good
god to be stronger than the evil god. These conceptions come
from the ancient Near East and have influenced our thinking in
the Church. We are not directly to be blamed for our naive trust
in the validity of these unbiblical thoughts, which are in fact
parts of Persian and other religions. We are not asked to believe
in Jesus Christ's power and in the power of Communism, in order
to make up our minds which of the two will be stronger in the
last analysis. This would pose impossible alternatives and it is
even sinful to draw the conclusion that we have to defend the
Christian Gospel against "other religions," or a "Christian country" against other powers, as if Jesus Christ had ever asked us
to defend Him or to consider other parts of the world as the
representatives of another god. There is no other god. A god
whom we can defend or even compare with powers in this world
is a self-constructed god, fitting perhaps to our ideas and fears;
he might be a god according to our needs, desires, and projec-
tions, but he is not the God whom we fear and love as the Father
of Jesus Christ, the Lord of Heaven and Earth. He will rather
be a god restricted and limited to the "other world," a god of
religion and religiosity, but not the God who in Jesus Christ
became flesh, was born of a woman, was born under Law, was
judged under the Law, and died in shame for our sakes. He
would be a god whom we could never reach, and not the God
of the Bible who has reached us in Jesus Christ.

To separate Jesus Christ from the world would be to lose both
Christ and the world. Dietrich Bonhoeffer calls this thinking in
two spheres "the colossal obstacle,"[31] and he summarizes it thus:
"So long as Christ and the world are conceived as two opposing
and mutually repellent spheres, man will be left in the following
dilemma: he abandons reality as a whole, and places himself in
one or other of the two spheres. He seeks Christ without the

[31] *Ethics* (New York: The Macmillan Company, 1955), p. 62.

world, or he seeks the world without Christ. In either case he is deceiving himself." The thinking in two spheres is "in profound contradiction to the thought of the Bible . . . There are not two realities, but only one reality, and that is the reality of God, which has become manifest in Christ in the reality of the world. Sharing in Christ we stand at once in both the reality of God and the reality of the world. The reality of Christ comprises the reality of the world within itself. The world has no reality of its own, independently of the revelation of God in Christ. One is denying the revelation of God in Jesus Christ if one tries to be 'Christian' without seeing and recognizing the world in Christ."[32]

All these statements and thoughts are necessary and vital for the faith of the Christian. They make it impossible to systematize the Christ event in terms of two categories or two worlds in such a way that Jesus Christ could be conceived as the ultimate reality of only one of them. But there is still another danger that one has to be aware of. To have escaped a logical or theological system, recognizing that it is unbiblical, does not mean that one is safe and speaks "Biblically" as long as he carefully avoids the false conclusions of that system. The Biblical statement, that we cannot have Christ without the world or the world without Christ, could also be turned into a system which automatically answers all the questions. This danger is already apparent in certain circles of ecumenical theology, and one has a certain right to be suspicious when it is noticed that it is great fashion to entitle conferences, magazines, and books with the words "Christ and World," or "The Church in the World," or with other words similar to these. Do the people in our churches really understand what we mean by it? And are we ourselves aware that these thoughts do not provide easy answers but rather confront us with the full depth and whole complexity of the Gospel?

The fact that the message of Christ must indeed be proclaimed in worldly words and secular language, even as the Lord Himself spoke the language of His worldly contemporaries, can

[32] *Ibid.*, p. 63-64.

under no circumstances mean that the *skandalon,* the stumbling block, of this message of the crucified Christ would become less offensive or could be minimized in any way. Just the contrary is true. The more we speak in churchly or even religious language, the more the real *skandalon* of the shameful Cross will be hidden and replaced by an unreal stumbling block of mere linguistic riddles. The more we speak the true and honest language of this world we live in, the more the real *skandalon* will be made known! The worldly and human language of the sermon of the saving and judging Word of God is the strongest and most direct way in which the living Christ wants to confront us. Our honest and genuine response to the claim of the Word of God must be a human and worldly response, and just in this way it will proclaim the humiliation and glorification of God even more clearly than any other language could ever do. Only a radical misunderstanding of the humanness of the Christian life and of the worldly words of the witness could suggest that the preacher should deliberately employ "worldly language" in accordance with psychological tricks or techniques in order to "reach" his people in a more clever and diplomatic way. The fact that our confessions and proclamations point to the worldly man Jesus, whom we confess to be the Messiah and Lord of the world, does not make preaching easier! It would be far easier to retreat to the sphere of religious expressions, symbols, and emotions. Every preacher will be constantly tempted to do this, especially when he is tired and overworked because of his routine work as a "professional proclaimer" week after week.

It is, therefore, the person and work of the witness which we have to examine on the subsequent pages. The problem is centered around the witness who points to Jesus Christ, because in Jesus Christ's election the witness has been called. Between Jesus Christ and His witness there is a strange and very intimate relation, which can certainly not be understood by someone who has not heard the witness. The words of the witness can only be understood in terms of the content of the witness. There are no outside proofs and guarantees.

4. THE WITNESS OF THE WORD

Man's call into "witness-ship" is grounded in the call of the first and true Witness of God, Jesus Christ. A witness (martys) *is a man before whose eyes God graciously performs His wonderful deeds; and a witness* (keryx) *is also a man who is commissioned by the risen Lord to cry out the coming of his Lord. The messengers of Christ have no credentials or outside proofs for the validity of their message. All they have is the content of their very message, which is Christ Himself. They are bound to the Word, which is also binding on others as soon as it is proclaimed.*

The work and the function of the witness according to the Old and New Testaments are usually interpreted in juridical and legal terms. The Biblical words *martyria* and *martys* must be interpreted with the awareness that they were originally merely technical terms in the language of the court and the law. The witness tells what he has seen; he testifies to what he has heard. It seems that the Greek word is connected with an indo-germanic root *smer,* which means something like "to remember, to think back, to recall,"[33] and it is even possible that the Latin word *memoria* is connected with this root. The witness, the *martys,* is the man who reports accurately to a court or a group of people what he has seen. The implication is that the event to which he is witnessing lies in the past. There is no doubt that the Bible uses the word in this sense. In order to guarantee that the validity of that to which one witnesses does not depend on the subjectivity of one person, two witnesses are required by the law. (Numbers 35:30; Deuteronomy 17:6; Matthew 18:16; Hebrews 10:28.) When there are personal difficulties within the Church, a Christian is to take another brother with him when he goes to discuss the issue with his opponent. (Matthew 18:16.) Jesus

[33] Gerhard Kittel (ed.), *Theologisches Wörterbuch zum Neuen Testament* (Stuttgart: W. Kohlhammer, 1942), Vol. IV, pp. 477-514.

Himself claims the double witness for His words (John 8:17-18);
Paul wants to discuss the differences with the Corinthians in the
presence of two or three of the brethren (2 Corinthians 13:1).
The witness must be true; life and death depend on it. A trans-
gression of the ninth commandment causes God's wrath upon
the false witnesses. The false witnesses against Jesus (Mark
14:55-60) and against Stephen (Acts 6:13) judge themselves.
If there were no second witness who could testify to the validity
of one's statement, or if one wanted to express something with
the claim of the utmost authority and truth, God Himself was
called upon to be a witness. (Jeremiah 42:5; Romans 1:9; 2 Corinthians 1:23; Philippians 1:8.) God the Father gives witness
to the Son, as the Son gives witness to the Father (John 5:30-32),
but also the works of Christ give witness to Him (John 5:36), as
do the Scriptures (John 5:39) and the Holy Spirit (John 15:26).
The acts of God are the content of the witness. The climax is
God's action in His Son Jesus Christ. Those who have seen His
glory are called to give witness to it. As the children of Israel
witness to the uniqueness of God (Isaiah 44:5-6), so the eye-
witnesses give witness to the crucifixion and resurrection of the
Lord. By making their witness, they not only give "reports" of
objective facts, but their very words of testimony are a claim
that the events to which they witness are the truth which they
themselves believe. One cannot separate an "objective" from a
"subjective" witness. The *martys*, the witness, testifies about the
event, and at the same time about the fact that he himself takes
the event as the absolute, binding truth — so much so that he is
prepared to die for it. For this reason the word *martyrium* and
its meaning in the Church are inseparably connected with the
work of the witness. The witness is prepared to become a martyr.

These statements are only a summary of more precise elaborations which can be found in special New Testament studies.
Since a "word study" never reveals the full meaning of a Biblical
word or thought, Biblical interpretation is not an accumulation
of word studies. When we examine the word "witness" (*martys*
or *martyria*) we do not necessarily find out what the content of

the witness is, and it goes without saying that this question is the most important of all. There is a danger in our churchly vocabulary that we use the word "witness" to indicate the person or the function of a person who "proclaims" the Good News of God in Christ to those who have not yet heard it. In other words, we identify "witness" with "proclamation." This identification is not quite correct, since a theological examination of the Biblical thoughts shows us that a witness is not primarily a man who says, proclaims, or speaks out what he has seen. A witness is first of all a man who sees. A witness is a man before whose eyes God graciously performs an action. God acts with His people Israel, and He acts in His Son Jesus Christ, and "we have beheld his glory, glory as of the only Son from the Father." (John 1:14.) God did not decide to perform His marvelous works in secrecy and privacy; He has called witnesses to see what He does, literally "to witness" the great deeds of God. It is premature pragmatism to say that "witness" is automatically identical with proclamation. There are witnesses of God's wonderful deeds, even if no one "bears a witness." God the Father, who has called His only Son to be our High Priest and King, has also called us to be the witnesses of these gracious acts. Everyone who hears the Word of God is a witness of it. Every Christian in the Church is a witness. But this does not mean that we can directly and mechanically conclude that everyone must go out into the world to "be a witness." He is already a witness before he goes out and professes to be one.

With this background, we can proceed to say that the call to be a witness of God's actions means that the witness cannot keep to himself what he has seen and heard; he must go out to tell the world. But even then we must be careful not to systematize the function of a witness. We have no right to deny that there are hours of proclamation and hours of silence. Nor would it make sense to speak of a "proclaiming silence;" silence is silence. If we understand our call into "witness-ship" as grounded in the call of the first and true Witness of God, Jesus Christ, we must realize that Jesus Christ speaks of hours of silence and patience. He can perform miracles and healings and tell the people involved to keep silence. To say that this was true only before Easter is not a sufficient explanation. The true reason for those hours of silence is rather that God wants us to know that we must wait for His command and appointment to go out as His messengers. The disciples of Christ, who are the true witnesses of God's great deeds, cannot be compared with the people who once learned a certain "doctrine" or ideology, which they now have to "spread out" with great intensity, and which only requires finding the appropriate psychological moment for proclamation. The proclamation of God's reconciling action in Jesus Christ is basically not a type of teaching or instruction which can be carried out practically at any time, provided that there are some people who are willing, or who can be "made willing," to listen. Here we have the dreadful warning, "Do not give dogs what is holy; and do not throw your pearls before swine, lest they trample them under foot and turn to attack you." (Matthew 7:6.) While it is true that all Christians are witnesses of God's merciful acts, it does not follow automatically that they have to preach these acts at every moment and to every group of people assembled.

Our analysis of the meaning of the word "witness" covers only one aspect of the full Biblical truth. The juridical and legal character of the original meaning of the word has made it quite clear that the witness says what he has seen in the past; i.e., the event to which he testifies has happened before he opens his mouth. The witness must look back to this event. This is really only one aspect of the function of the witness. If we built our total understanding of preaching and proclaiming on this conception, we would be in danger of turning the Gospel into an ideology, a doctrine, a philosophy of history, or a *Corpus Christianum* — a complex of Christian truths, which can be taught and explained at all times and to all people, provided they are intelligent enough and willing to listen.

Such proclamation could as well be done in the absence of Jesus Christ as in His presence. "Teaching Christianity" is perfectly possible without Jesus Christ. His presence is not necessary, and it could even be disturbing to our goal of teaching, expounding, or propagating interpretations of historical events which happened long ago. The statement, "This do in remembrance of me," is a perfectly "orthodox" sentence, which theoretically points to the death and resurrection of Jesus Christ. It is in a way a "witness." So are many other Biblical or "orthodox" quotations and statements. It is quite legitimate to quote the Bible or the outstanding and generally accepted confessions of the Church, as they are authentic witnesses to God's action in Jesus Christ. But no critically thinking Christian will conclude that those quotations and repetitions are automatically the *martyria,* the witness of which the New Testament is speaking. Repetitions and theoretical expositions of the witness of other Christians are the perfect caricature of the Biblical understanding of witnessing. "Therefore, behold, I am against the prophets, says the Lord, who steal my words from one another." (Jeremiah 23:30.)

It is the presence of the risen Christ that makes a human witness a real witness. It is the claim, call, and royal command that authorizes the witness to speak the Word of the Lord. The Bible, therefore, uses besides the word *martys,* witness, the word *keryx,* herald. The herald is the witness who goes out as a messenger to proclaim and announce in the streets and market places the coming of his king. His message is urgent; it cannot even be taught, for it must be cried out. It is cried out in the authority of Christ the coming King. The call of the herald is a call for decision (in this and perhaps only in this context can we use this dangerous word). "Today, when you hear his voice, do not harden your hearts." (Hebrews 4:7.) The Christian herald cannot give his own interpretation and opinion; he must say what his King wants him to say. The words of a herald are not an explication of his own theology or a confession of his own experience and Christian life. All these activities have their own proper place: interpretation and advice in the hours of pastoral care; exposition and explication in the hours of teaching; candid confession and exchange of experience in the quiet hours of complete openness among friends. But all this is not preaching, for it is not the public service of the herald for the King. It was Kierkegaard who recalled for the theologians the difference between an "apostle and a genius." The genius is qualified to speak because of his birth, education, and self-discipline, but the apostle is commissioned to speak for another. The herald receives the revelation and is called to be used as the mouthpiece of God's voice.[34] He cannot be replaced by the religious or philosophical genius who can only speak in his own authority. The herald speaks in the authority of his Lord: "Behold, I have put my words in your mouth." (Jeremiah 1:9.) The preacher cannot want to be understood as a genius in communication, presentation, and application of the Gospel. He would be fighting against his own calling, should he desire to reach perfection in these techniques. Time and again he will be tempted to concentrate on technique, and he will buy books which bear ambiguous and promising titles because he seems to feel that the people in the church want him to be an eloquent genius in interpretation and presentation. There is indeed an inclination to prefer an *authoritarian* preacher to an *authoritative* preacher. This is a quite natural and very honest reaction of the world, which frequently knows more honesty than the Church; for the world wants to have proof and a guarantee for the witness of the herald. The world does not want to give itself up so soon after having heard a message which challenges all its conceptions. It wants to hear preachers who know how to persuade people; preachers who are masters at minimizing the *skandalon* of the challenging Word of God; preachers who make it easier to become Christians. Even if the preacher wants to escape this diabolical temptation, he will constantly find himself in the neighborhood of the false prophets, who speak in their own name and proclaim their own wisdom. By the majority of his hearers he will be taken as a man who speaks in his own authority and out of his own wisdom, for the world cannot conceive of the possibility of a preacher whose

[34] Cf. Richardson, *op. cit.*, ch. 13, "The Apostolic and Priestly Ministry."

authority is not in himself. It will always be this way, because
the heralds of God have no outside proof for the validity of their
message. "But behold, they will not believe me or listen to my
voice, for they will say, 'The LORD did not appear to you.'"
(Exodus 4:1.) The herald of God has nothing but the Word on
which to rely. He is called in Jesus Christ and authorized by
Him; he has His Word and nothing else to support his legiti-
macy. He shares this situation with Jesus, his master, whose
words were only verified by themselves: "he who receives his
testimony sets his seal to this, that God is true." (John 3:33.)
It is illogical but very Biblical to say that the Word of the Lord
is verified by the Word of the Lord. Rudolf Bultmann expresses
it this way, "The paradox is that the word of Jesus does not find
its substantiation by a backward movement from the attesting
word to the thing attested — as it might if the thing itself were
confirmable irrespective of the word — but finds it only in a
faith-prompted acceptance of the word."[35] It has often been said
(because of 2 Corinthians 5:20) that the heralds of Christ are
"ambassadors," but the ambassadors of this world have their
credentials which they can and must present to the monarch
or president of the nation to which they come. The messengers
of Christ have no such credentials — all they have is the content
of their very message, which is Jesus Christ Himself. They are
completely bound to the Word, which is also binding on others
as soon as it is proclaimed. This is the reason for the strange
solidarity[36] between the heralds of Christ and the unbelievers:
as soon as the herald begins to speak, both the herald and the
hearers are under the authority of the Word! It can only be
understood if we keep firmly in mind that it is the presence of
the living Christ Himself that gives authority and power to the
message of His heralds. Therefore, the heralds can never per-

[35] *Theology of the New Testament* (New York: Charles Scribner's Sons,
1955), Vol. II, p. 68.
[36] Cf. Markus Barth, *op. cit.*, pp. 154-169: "Solidarity: sinners and saved
together." This chapter is one of the clearest Biblical expositions of the
question of Church and World in recent theological literature made available for nontheologians.

form their work according to principles or rules, which could very well apply for representatives of firms, political parties, or religions. The heralds of Christ are directly under the command of the message they have to convey. They cannot be slower or faster in the progress of their work than the Word is; they cannot try to reach more people than the Word reaches; they cannot prepare people in order to reach them with the Word at a later date. Furthermore, they cannot withdraw if the Word is defeated and despised; the Word is with them and they will also be defeated and despised. This is not just a possibility; it is rather the very concrete prophecy and promise of Christ. The messengers will suffer with Him. "Then they will deliver you up to tribulation, and put you to death; and you will be hated by all nations for my name's sake." (Matthew 24:9.) The royal word of comfort, "see that you are not alarmed" (Matthew 24:6), can be understood only on ground of the promise that it is the living God Himself who acts with and through His heralds. "When they deliver you up, do not be anxious how you are to speak or what you are to say; for what you are to say will be given to you in that hour; for it is not you who speak, but the Spirit of your Father speaking through you." (Matthew 10:19-20.)[37]

God's offer of forgiveness and new life has been made in Jesus Christ at a certain time and for all times. There is no part of the world, nor is there any religion or political ideology, which is too far away or too sinful for that offer. When the Church confesses with the New Testament that God reconciled the world to Himself "once and for all," the Church does not mean by this that God intends, plans, or desires to do it, but it confesses that He has already done so. Here is the message of the heralds. Perhaps we are accustomed to thinking of a "herald" as a man who arrives at a given destination a certain time before

[37] This is a passage which indicates clearly that the life in the Church is the *proprium* of the Holy Spirit (cf. pp. 30 ff.); it is not a mystical or spiritualized Christ in whom we are called to believe, but here Jesus speaks clearly about God the Holy Spirit.

his master and king will arrive at that place, which indicates that our picture language and our metaphors are somewhat insufficient. The Biblical messenger is not only to be understood as a man who announces something which is to come, but his very arrival is itself the advent of the things he announces. "He who hears you hears me, and he who rejects you rejects me, and he who rejects me rejects him who sent me." (Luke 10:16.) The "presence of Christ" with the messenger is not only a spiritualistic or subjective "feeling of presence" to strengthen the herald. In very plain language, Jesus Christ is "really present" when His Word is proclaimed by His messenger. He is "objectively" there, not only for the mind and the imagination of the messenger, but also for the hearers. The word of the messenger is not a preparation for a more powerful Word which Jesus might speak at a later date. Jesus Christ speaks in the Holy Spirit through the mouth of His witness; He works through His witnesses. (Romans 15:18; 1 Corinthians 15:10.) The Word of God in Christ is on the lips of the human heralds. This is the worldliness of the Word, which is the Word of the ultimate authority. We hear, however, the promise of ultimate fulfillment and the glorious establishing of the New World, but it would surely be wrong to devaluate for this reason the authority of God's heralds in our time! The same God who speaks to us now will speak at the Last Day. But at that time there will no longer be witness, preaching, and prayer; we will then see "face to face."

It has been necessary to see together the two Biblical words "witness" and "herald" (martys and keryx). We cannot afford to operate with only one of them, lest we turn to certain types of sects, which either systematize the word "witness" or make a philosophy of the function of the herald. The variety of errors in this connection is almost endless. One must see the full width of the Biblical words in order to understand that the proclamation of the Church is martyria: witness of God's deeds, which happened once and for all, and also words of the risen Jesus Christ who speaks now through the mouth of His heralds. (In the New Testament this is sometimes summarized with the noun form *kerygma*, but certainly not so frequently as to justify using it as a theological catchword.) The two expressions reflect the tension and unity between the "once and for all" acts of God, on the one hand, and God's constant presence and preservation of the Church through Jesus Christ in His Spirit, on the other hand.

The work of the obedient witness is grounded in the work of Jesus Christ. Jesus Christ calls and appoints him and gives him authority by being with him. When the witness loses sight of the work of Jesus Christ, he may speak and witness as "orthodoxly" as he possibly can, but his words will not be authoritative. It is only by following Jesus Christ in His human and humble way of sacrifice and humiliation that the words of the witness can be true words of response. "For to this you have been called, because Christ also suffered for you, leaving you an example, that you should follow in his steps." (1 Peter 2:21.) It should not be impossible to make a simple statement in order to clarify all this: God has spoken to us in Jesus; Jesus is His Word to us; Jesus is obedient to the Father on our behalf; because of the manhood of the ascended Christ, we can, in Him, follow His call and be with Him and share His obedience, for He has been elected eternally to fulfill what we ought to be; our answer to His demand can and must be given in a way that corresponds to His own human and worldly Word; our words will then be words of authority.

One of the leading thoughts in this chapter has been the understanding of the importance of the eternal election of Jesus, the first and true Witness, in relation to our work as witnesses and heralds. Our call, work, and words cannot be separated from His call, work, and Word. In order to prevent misunderstandings, it must finally be said that there is no such thing as a "neutral call," i.e., a call as such. The prophets were not called for the purpose of being called only. Nor are the disciples called for the purpose of leaving the world in order to "be with Christ." The witnesses are called and sent at the same time. The Church does not have a mission, but the Church *is* a mission. Her Lord is a Lord of calling and of sending. Although many Biblical thoughts can be graphically illustrated, this one certainly cannot — that God calls in Jesus Christ witnesses to His Glory, and that this call means at the same time that they are sent out into the world. The witness must become a herald, and if not a herald who is now commanded to speak, then a laborer in the harvest who must be ready at any time to speak the Word which he receives. That means in any case that the call to come to Jesus Christ is a call to go into the world. In this way the disciples do what Jesus Christ has already done: "As the Father has sent me, even so I send you." (John 20:21.) There is no obedient work other than participation in the obedience of Jesus Christ.

5. THE SERMON IS THE WORD OF GOD

There is an analogy between the conception of the sermon as God's Word and the Bible as God's Word. Both are statements of faith. One depends upon the other. The logical contradiction that the sermon creates the Church, and that the Church creates the sermon, must be seen in the light of the logical contradiction that Jesus Christ is the exalted Lord and the humiliated man of Nazareth. It is because of the free gift of His presence that the sermon can become the Word of God.

Human witness and confession consists in thankful and grateful pointing to the confession God has made in Jesus Christ. By giving the life of His only begotten Son, He has confessed that He loves the world and the sinful people in it. Preaching is to say this with all the consequences and radical implications, which are indeed contrary to the expectations and speculations of men. It should now be clear that preaching is not done by virtue of one's own enthusiasm or in the power of one's own name or authority, but by virtue of our call and in the power of His name and authority. It can happen through the grace of God that our human words are of no less authority than His own Word. His Word becomes our word. Paul writes to the Thessalonians, "And we also thank God constantly for this, that when you received the word of God which you heard from us, you accepted it not as the word of men but as what it really is, the word of God, which is at work in you believers." (1 Thessalonians 2:13.)

We have seen that the human word of the witness can only be the Word of God through the presence of Jesus Christ in the Holy Spirit. This is not just a "theological formula." If we left it out, we would have a Word of God that is separated from God; we would make God the prisoner of our thoughts or theologies. We would have a Word with which we could operate, a Word we could "use," a Word we could judge. But it could not be the Word of God, the Word which operates with us, uses us, and judges us. Our work in the Church, therefore, can only be a service to this one life-giving Word of God. The clearest expression of this truth is the fact that there is no other way to preach than to preach an "expository sermon,"[38] and even this is not a guarantee. All the members of the Church participate in Christ's office of self-proclamation. A preacher as a single individual cannot usurp this gift for himself by claiming that he and he alone can exegete the Bible and therefore preach it with authority. The authority of Christ's presence is a gift given to the whole Church. This gift demands the response of prayer and obedience of all the members of the Church. The simple "technique" of preaching an expository sermon does not force Christ to be present or to authorize the word of the preacher. The whole congregation stands in the vicariate, or "succession," as Karl Barth calls it,[39] which is not a succession of offices or qualities, but a succession of the proclamation, which can only happen because of the presence of the risen Lord in the Church.

[38] There is some confusion concerning the terms. The expressions "expository," "exegetical," and "textual" preaching represent by now almost three different ways of preaching, although it is impossible, reading the homiletical literature, to define the exact meaning of these types of sermons. It would be far simpler to use all of them with the same meaning.

[39] *Church Dogmatics*, Vol. I, Part 1, p. 106 ff., 116 ff.

The Word rules over the Church, and the Church is called to hear, accept, and proclaim it; it can never be inverted so that the Church rules over the Word. We cannot even say that the Church "has the Word;" this kind of expression should not be used in theological books, essays, or especially in our local churches. It is a miracle, which cannot be explained and summarized in principles and systems, that Jesus Christ, the Lord of the Church, promises to be *with* the Church "always, to the close of the age." (Matthew 28:20.) The boundaries of the Church are unknown to herself. She is the ever growing and moving action of God's self-manifestation upon earth. The Church makes manifest the love of her Lord, and she can do this only because of His presence.

What then is the relation between the Church and the sermon, if we assume that the sermon is truly based on a passage of the Bible? Two answers present themselves. First, the sermon is the Word of God because it is based on the Biblical witness, which points directly to God's acts in Christ. The sermon is therefore the Word which comes from God to the Church. The sermon confronts the Church. The sermon comes from the outside and brings the life, light, and truth of God. The sermon creates new hearts and new lives; the sermon creates the Church. Second, the sermon is the Word of God because it is based on the Biblical witness, but also because the preacher and all those who helped him to understand the Bible passage for his sermon were already members of the Church. Without a Church that enables people to be preachers, a sermon is quite unthinkable. The preacher was brought up in the Church, educated by the Church or at least influenced by books written by churchmen, and his Sunday sermon is only possible because he was already a member of the Church on Saturday. The Church, therefore, creates the sermon.

These two answers are really opposed to each other. The same dilemma appears in a different form in the controversy with the Roman Catholic Church with regard to the question of the canon. The Roman Church claims that the Church of Jesus

Christ existed before the Bible came into existence; hence, they conclude, the Bible was created by the Church and there is no reason whatsoever to see a break between the Bible and the tradition of the Church. What do we answer? We will admit that the Church existed before the Bible did, and we will also admit that the Biblical books were written by members of the Early Church. But we will not agree that "the Bible," as distinct from "tradition," was created by the Church. We will claim that the canon of the New Testament was recognized by the Church because of the witness which was to be heard *from* these books. In other words, we point back to the One to whom the books of the Bible witness. By saying this we state that Jesus Christ is the final authority who can be heard in these of men. This is a daring statement, which is rightly called a decision of faith.[40] It means that we admit that the Biblical books were written by normal human beings, and yet we maintain that their writings were recognized by the Early Church as true voices of witnesses pointing to the divine Word made flesh in Jesus Christ. We agree with the decision made in faith by the early Christians that there is nothing outside of the witness which can tell us anything about the validity of the witness, but that the witness itself is sufficient. We recognize the second form of the Word of God in the written form of the Old and New Testaments, and not *outside* of these books, and we do this only because we have heard what is inside these books of the Bible.

There is an obvious analogy between the conception of the sermon as God's Word and the Bible as God's Word. Both are statements of faith. Without these statements, thinking about the Bible, as well as about preaching, would become very difficult, if not impossible. We are not willing to say that the written witness of the Biblical books can be superseded by any other written witnesses which could constitute the Church and its

[40] Karl Barth, *op. cit.*, Vol. I, Part 2, p. 537: "Scripture is recognized as the Word of God by the fact that it *is* the Word of God." It is at this "weakest point" of Protestant theology, "where it can only acknowledge and confess," that "it has all its indestructible strength."

faith; nor do we want to say that the acting of Christ through the Holy Spirit in the sermon could be superseded by any other function or action. The Roman Church disagrees with these statements, hence it must think differently about the sermon. For the Roman Church the sermon can only be participation in or continuation of the work of the Fathers. In our theology in the Protestant Churches, the thinking about the canon is more settled than that about preaching. However, one depends upon the other. In either case it is a question of the self-evidence of the Word of God: for the canon, the second form; and for preaching, the first form of the Word of God. It is one and the same Word of God in both cases, so that the problem of the canon cannot be separated from the problem of preaching. The uncertainty about the analogy between the problem of the canon and the problem of the understanding of the proclaimed form of the Word of God is certainly the reason for so much confusion and so many differences concerning the definitions of preaching and worship.

The two contradictory answers to our question about the relation between the Church and the sermon are in fact only another way of putting the Christological analogy. The sermon comes "from the outside" to the Church and creates life, because of the Lordship of the exalted Christ who cares for His Church, and who protects and guides it to perfection. But it is also true that the sermon is "made" by the Church, and that we cannot think about a sermon without thinking about a Church out of which the sermon, or at least the preacher and the hearers, could come. This is true because of the Incarnation and the ministry of Christ, who is beside us, working on our behalf. But one must say more than this. This analogy cannot be a "static system,"[41] as if God's acting with His people happened outside the order of time. There is a definite priority. God speaks first, and then things come into being. God calls a man, puts His words into his mouth, and only then is he a prophet. Jesus calls His disciples, and only then can they go out with His authority.

[41] Cf. pp. 47-48.

God calls the witnesses of the Resurrection, and they and their followers respond to it by writing the books which we now find in the Bible. In short, God's Word has priority, and only after God has spoken can men respond. Likewise the sermon has priority over the existence of the congregation, even if a young candidate preached his first sermon to a congregation of old and experienced members. Of course in the case of preaching, the priority is not a chronological one, but it is based on the priority and authority of the Word of God itself, which is also, as far as time and chronology are concerned, the first event that ever happened. It was first of all God Himself who decided in His mercy to perform His creating work, and therefore to speak to His creatures with His Word, which was made flesh and came to us in Jesus of Nazareth. Our response is caused by His call. With this understanding, it must be maintained that the sermon has absolute priority over the congregation, but this priority does not exclude the active work of the congregation for the "production" of a sermon; on the contrary, it includes it. The Word creates life; it calls labor, work, and activity into existence. The life and activity created by the Word cannot possibly be dead and passive! The Church which is fed by the Word will begin to work and to make manifest God's love to which it owes its existence. The Church not only takes a certain part in the proclamation, but it is also the very instrument of proclamation! We are not to think of the priority of the sermon as if each Sunday's sermon would "establish" the Church anew, or as if the preacher were to think that all his people had lost their faith completely during the week, and that he had to preach to ice-cold unbelievers. The Holy Spirit is at work during the week preceding the sermon; or should the preacher distrust the authority of last Sunday's sermon? The Word of the sermon is indeed a new Word and not a repetition of last Sunday's sermon, but this does not mean that each sermon devaluates or extinguishes the previous sermons. If this were so, the New Testament could never speak about a "Church" and Paul could never refer to the message he had brought before. But this is exactly what the New Testament does, and it even claims that all present and future proclamations must be based on the proclamation of the prophets and apostles, and on the *evangel,* which has created life and faith. "But even if we, or an angel from heaven, should preach to you a gospel contrary to that which we preached to you, let him be accursed." (Galatians 1:8.) This is true because Jesus Christ's presence among His people does not consist of appearances discontinuous in time, i.e., which occur only here and there for a little while, so that He would disappear leaving the Church lonely and forgotten until a brave preacher decided to preach another sermon.

This double aspect of the sermon, which on the one hand indeed creates the Church and on the other hand is also the work of the Church, reflects the fact that the Church lives in time and not in eternity. The Church has a history with which it is in solidarity. The Church has a "yesterday" as much as it has a today and a tomorrow. These are the times of Jesus Christ, in whom the Church is elected and in whom it lives. He is the same all the time. The witness which pointed to him yesterday cannot be abolished, least of all the Biblical witness which has absolute priority over other voices (which all depend on the Biblical witness). Nevertheless, the Word, in which Christ meets us again and again, is each time a new Word. His grace is new every morning; it cannot be caught up in principles, statements, persons, consecrated buildings, or objects (e.g., the elements of the Lord's Supper). The continuity between yesterday and today lies purely in the person of Christ Himself and never in our human response. This conception is very necessary for the understanding of the relation between the Old and the New Testaments.

It is Jesus Christ's self-revelation, His will and activity, that causes the Biblical witness to break through to a new and living witness. This is the meaning of the term "the self-will of the Biblical text."[42] This term, although a bit ugly, is a helpful abbreviation in homiletical thinking, for it expresses the fact that

[42] Cf. p. 46.

it is Christ Himself who is His own Evangelist and Preacher. The task of the Church, and primarily of the preacher, is to listen to the Biblical text, so that the voice of that text, namely Christ Himself, can be heard. Paul, who could have been under the suspicion that he only reproduced what Ananias had told him (Acts 9:10-22), expressed it this way, "For I would have you know, brethren, that the gospel which was preached by me is not man's gospel. For I did not receive it from man, nor was I taught it, but it came through a revelation of Jesus Christ." (Galatians 1:11-12.) The living voice of the Gospel, the *viva vox evangelii*, breaks through the human words of the witnesses, and it is this living voice which must be heard if the sermon is to be a sermon. If the preacher and his co-workers[43] cannot hear this voice in their preparation for the sermon on the coming Sunday, they have either failed to translate, read, exegete, and pray as they ought to have, or they may have chosen the wrong text. To speak about the latter possibility is, of course, very dangerous; this question will be discussed in another section.[44] If, however, the living voice is heard and preached in close attention and obedience to the passage which is the sermon text, then it is Christ Himself who speaks. The human witness is then, as it is said of Paul, an instrument of Christ's self-proclamation; "he is a chosen instrument of mine to carry my name before the Gentiles and kings and the sons of Israel" (Acts 9:15), a man in whose mouth God has put His words (Jeremiah 1:9). "Not that we are sufficient of ourselves to claim anything as coming from us; our sufficiency is from God, who has qualified us to be ministers of a new covenant, not in a written code but in the Spirit." (2 Corinthians 3:5-6.) Now we can understand why the daring statement of the Second Helvetic Confession (1566) can be made: "Wherefore when this Word of God is now preached in the church by preachers lawfully called, we believe that the very Word of God is preached, and

[43] To the necessity of corporate sermon preparation, cf. pp. 123 ff., 133-134, 153-157.
[44] Cf. pp. 149-157, 160-162.

received of the faithful; and that neither any other Word of
God is to be feigned, nor to be expected from heaven: and
that now the Word itself which is preached is to be regarded,
not the minister that preaches; who, although he be evil and
a sinner, nevertheless the Word of God abides true and good."[45]
True respect is paid to God by putting oneself under the judgment of a human sermon, even if the human being who preaches
that sermon is "an evil man and a sinner" *(etsi sit malus et
peccator)!* We cannot promise the congregation that they will
hear a better word and a stronger voice than our own weak,
sinful, and human sermon. We have no right to wait for a voice
from heaven to confirm positively that the words of our preachers
were not too bad. Least of all can we put our trust in candles,
altars, and symbols to guarantee, so to speak "from the outside,"
that the human and imperfect sermons were preached in the
right context and in the environment of the authority of the
Church. It is in the weakness of the human word that God confronts us with Himself, and we would miss the point completely
if we were to understand this as an unfortunate and special
burden for our faith. The very contrary is true: it is because of
God's infinite mercy and wisdom that He has chosen our human
words to make Himself known to us. If He had decided to speak
otherwise, we would not be able to understand Him and to
respond to His claim and offer. In this mystery of God's humiliation in Jesus Christ, we submit ourselves by humbly confessing
that it is precisely in the human and worldly word of the sermon
that the eternal God speaks to us. Martin Luther grew so accustomed to this manner of thinking that he usually called the
sermon simply the "Word of God." In a passage which is frequently quoted, he says, "A preacher must not pray the Lord's
prayer, nor must he ask for forgiveness of sins after he has
preached (if he is a true preacher). But he must say with
Jeremiah and boast: 'Lord, thou knowest that which came out
of my lips was before thy face.' And with Paul and all apostles

[45] Philip Schaff (ed.), *The Creeds of Christendom,* 4th ed. (New York:
Harper & Brothers, 1919), Vol. III, p. 832.

and prophets can he be comforted and say: *Haec dixit dominus.* (This has God himself spoken.) *Et iterum.* I have been an apostle and prophet of Jesus Christ in this sermon. Here it is not necessary — and not even good — to ask for forgiveness of sins, as if it had been falsely taught. Because it is God's word and not mine, which God need not and cannot forgive me, but rather confirms, praises, and crowns; and He must say to me: you have rightly taught, for I have spoken through you, and the Word is mine. Those who cannot say this about their sermon, had better not preach."[46] Karl Barth quotes this passage after having quoted a similar passage in one of Calvin's sermons on the opening verses of Galatians, and confesses that he had thought when writing his early Prolegomena that this passage in Luther was unacceptable, but has now changed his mind.[47] It is indeed the most daring statement about preaching which we can make, and we can make it only on the grounds of the union with Christ. In Him has been done what is impossible for men: that God and man come together in Jesus Christ. Christ is delivered into the hands of man and dies on the Cross; and it is exactly this Word of the Cross which comes through the mouth of man, who is made a new man by the resurrection of Christ. If we lose sight of the crucified and risen Lord, and if we examine our own abilities as preachers and speakers (and expect to find the secret of preaching in the art of communication and presentation), then of course it is impossible to believe the statement of the Second Helvetic Confession or the passage in Luther. It is only in Jesus Christ that we can and must make this statement. There is no compromise and no middle ground. The sermon is either the Word of God, or it is nothing but reflection and meditation. But meditations and opinions would never justify our publicly inviting people of all nations, races, and ages to attend church services to listen to our sermons. They could never be words of death and life. "For we are the

[46] "Wider Hans Worst," 1541, *Weimarer Ausgabe* 51, 517; or *Clemen IV*, p. 347; my translation.
[47] Karl Barth, *op. cit.*, Vol. I, Part 2, p. 747.

aroma of Christ to God among those who are being saved and among those who are perishing, to one a fragrance from death to death, to the other a fragrance from life to life. Who is sufficient for these things? For we are not, like so many, peddlers of God's Word; but as men of sincerity, as commissioned by God, in the sight of God we speak in Christ." (2 Corinthians 2:15-17.)

It is obviously not very satisfying to use the Lutheran formula "in, with, and under" in order to express *how* the Word of God is connected with the human word of the human witness. These three terms have never really clarified the question of *how* Christ is present in the Lord's Supper, and they will hardly perform a better service when we employ them for the understanding of the sermon. The presence of Jesus Christ cannot be described otherwise than by words of response which point to His presence. Furthermore, those words of response cannot be formulated once and for all. We have seen earlier that the content of the witness can only be examined and understood by listening to the witness, and this is analogically true for the presence of Christ. The presence is the gift of grace, the fulfillment of the promise, the answer to our prayers, and it is above all the free action of God in Christ. It cannot be described or caught up in formulas, for there is no automatic identification between our sermon and the Word of God. The presence of Christ in the sermon is nothing less than the presence of the eternal Father who speaks in Jesus Christ through the Holy Spirit His very own Word of judgment and consolation, life and light; but it happens according to the secret of the *ubi et quando visum est deo,* the free decision of God to reveal Himself wherever and whenever He decides. The identification between God's Word and the word of the human witness is under no circumstances the work of man, but always the free work of God.

The sermon is, therefore, an action of God in Christ through the Holy Spirit with the people who are rightly called the *communio sanctorum,* the communion of saints. They serve the God who acts. They respond to Him, but it is God who calls.

He addresses all of them, and all of them are called to respond. This, of course, raises serious questions concerning the understanding of our worship services and their liturgical forms. They must now be examined in the following chapter. Only after having thought about the questions regarding the Church — its liturgy, its offices, and its life — can we proceed to the more detailed implications of the sermon and its preparation.

II Worship
and the Office of Proclamation

1. THE DIFFICULTY OF FINDING
AN EXEGETICAL BASIS FOR WORSHIP

The New Testament does not provide concrete answers to the questions concerning the form and the parts of the early Christian worship. Constitutive of worship is the assembly of the believers; it is the exalted Christ who works through the Holy Spirit, and who forms the believers into His own body. Inasmuch as the death and resurrection of Christ is for all people, it is the totality of the people in the Church who participate actively with their gifts of grace during the hour of worship. There is no auditorium — all are on the stage.

It is interesting to observe that the ministers and church members in our time are far more concerned with the questions of worship, liturgy, church life, and church government than with the Biblical and dogmatical questions which arise out of our Bible study. A newly appointed minister will often have made up his mind to change this or that part of the order of worship before he really begins to know the congregation and to work in it. He will have to face opposition if he wants to abolish a part of the order of service or to introduce something new. A change of the liturgy, music, architecture, and government of the church will cause infinitely more discussion than this or that dogmatical statement. How true this is can be proved by the experiment of trying to decide to which denomination a preacher belongs when one listens with closed eyes or hears a sermon preached on the radio. Almost any congregation will tolerate a docetic, an ebionitic, a gnostic, a synergistic, or even

79

a philosophical sermon, as well as almost any interpretation of
a Biblical text, and even sermons without any Biblical founda-
tion at all. But not so when it comes to questions of church
government or forms of worship.[1] The differences between denominations were at one time firmly based on Biblical interpretations. The "doctrine" of justification, eschatology, the Lord's
Supper, the order of worship, and the government of the Church
literally constituted denominations, and these important questions were inseparably connected with the exegesis of Genesis,
Isaiah, Romans, Galatians, John's Apocalypse, 1 Corinthians,
the Pastoral Epistles, etc. In our time, however, most church
members have lost sight of the Biblical and doctrinal roots of
their denominations. Instead there is a predominant interest in
the outward forms of worship, in the church furniture and the
arrangement of it, and in the form of the government of the
church. These fixed ideas cause more difficulties in ecumenical
work than the questions of whether we are willing to accept the
doctrine of the three forms of the Word of God, or whether we
are ready to say with Luther and the other Reformers that the
exalted Christ Himself speaks in our worship services through
the mouth of His servants, or whether we formulate Christology
and the doctrine of the Trinity in this or that way. The giving
up of hallowed traditions is a far greater obstacle to Intercommunion and church union than the changing of dogmatic
and exegetical views. What constituted the distinctive characteristics of the various denominations at the time of the Reformation
has been pushed into the background, and the secondary results
of these conceptions have been moved into the foreground. A
Biblical scholar in one denomination will be more in agreement
with his colleague in another denomination than with his
brethren in his own denomination who do not share his concern
for Biblical studies.

[1] Cf. the distressing absence of dogmatical and Biblical arguments in the
congregation's reactions to the proposals concerning Intercommunion between the Church of Scotland and the Church of England. No matter
where one's sympathy lies, it is impossible to decide the questions on merely
"practical" grounds.

The Bible looks in the opposite direction, so that what the Biblical texts say about the order of worship and the form of government of the Church is very uncertain and in many ways ambiguous. One can prove almost anything, or at least say many things that cannot be challenged, by the exegesis of the Bible. However, the Biblical texts speak clearly and unambiguously about revelation, reconciliation, the work of the exalted Christ in the Holy Spirit, and the relation of Christians to the world. The Biblical witnesses have a burning interest in these central issues, and they want to reach, as far as possible, clarity and understanding among all Christians. The prophetic and apostolic witness does not allow us to take the Good News of the Bible for granted, or to hand over the thinking about it to the "dogmaticians" of the Church, so as to make us free and safe to spend our time in thinking and talking about liturgy, pastoral counseling, the art of communication, or church administration. A short investigation of the New Testament conception of worship will demonstrate how difficult it is to reach a clear understanding of the "ideal" form of worship.

The New Testament writers might have chosen to use the familiar Greek words for "worship," "sacrifice," and "liturgy" for the description of their own Christian worship services, as these terms were used by the Greek-speaking groups of the mystery religions. But this is exactly what they did not do, for they did not want to be mixed up with these religious groups. They knew and employed the old Greek words, but with completely new connotations. The words for "worship," "sacrifice," etc., were used rather for the totality of the everyday Christian life. The New Testament abolished the pagan distinction between the holy hours of mystical union with the godhead during the service and the dead, empty, and sinful days of duty during the week. The service (latreia) is done by all the brethren, not only during the hours of worship, but also as the obedient function of their whole lives. (Romans 12:1.) The liturgy (leiturgia) was originally a service or a work on behalf of the people to whom the liturgist belongs; it is now the work of prayer, or service in general, of the apostolic mission, and even of the work of Christ Himself, as well as the work of Epaphroditus, who brings the gifts of the Philippians to Paul (Philippians 2:25), and thus the *leiturgia* of the Philippians to Paul (Philippians 2:30). Likewise the word "sacrifice" *(thysia)* is not restricted to a cultic function, but goes far beyond this conception to cover the whole service of the people in the Church.

What, then, is the criterion for the worship service of the New Testament community? The early Christians changed the meaning of the technical terms for "worship" and "sacrifice," for they wanted to see their whole lives under these titles. They even introduced a new word, which had no relation to cultic worship services at all, namely *diakonia*. But even this word, which they preferred to the other more familiar expressions, is not used in the New Testament for "worship services" as such, for it also covers the whole field of service in the world. Then what is the word or the idea that denotes a proper worship service? We are almost left in the dark when we try to find a Biblical answer to this question, for we cannot find a "theological" term or name for the hour of worship in the whole of the New Testament. The only words which offer some help are *ekklesia*, usually translated "church," and *synerchesthai* or *synagesthai*, which are sometimes rendered in the Vulgate by the Latin verbs *congregare* and *convenire*. These two Latin words show very clearly that the meaning of the Greek verbs is the "congregation" or the "convent," i.e., the coming together in the assembly of the believers, which is what constitutes an hour of worship service! The word *ekklesia* supports this understanding, for only very seldom does it mean "church" in the general sense. In most of the more than eighty occurences in the New Testament it points to the actual gathering or assembly of the believers. We can, therefore, say that the only certain answer which comes from the Biblical texts is that the assembly of believers was necessary for a worship service: no assembly — no worship service. The difference between the service, sacrifice, and liturgy during the week and the hour of worship on Sunday (or on another day) is the simple fact that the believers are gathered together.

Of course this conclusion is only the result of a word study. After having seen that the New Testament refuses to give another answer to our question concerning the criterion of a worship service, we can still approach the texts with a second question: What actually happened during these hours while they were gathered? We hear of prayers (1 Corinthians 14:14-16; Acts 6:6; etc.), and in particular of the Lord's Prayer and the doxology added to it as a response by the congregation. We know of early forms of eucharistic prayers and liturgical prayers (1 Clement 59-61), and we can still find short forms of confessions,[2] although we are not quite sure whether they really belonged to the corporate worship or only to the baptismal instructions. But Didache 14:1 says that there were also confessions of sin, and we find parts of hymns (Philippians 2:6-11; etc.) and references to hymns (1 Corinthians 14:26; Colossians 3:16; etc.). We hear of preaching, teaching, prophecy, speaking in tongues and the interpretation of it. We read of benedictions and references to benedictions; we hear of the collection of money (1 Corinthians 16:2; Acts 5:1-11) and of the utterances of people who had a "grace gift." And above all, we have direct and hidden references in the Gospels and in many of the Epistles to the Lord's Supper.

It is not impossible to reach detailed results and concrete definitions by careful exegesis and comparison of the many passages which mention directly or indirectly parts of the worship services of the early Christians. But we are not sure how many of these actions and functions were necessary for a worship service. We do not even know whether the early Christians had special rooms or buildings for their meetings. It does seem to be clear that they worshiped on the Lord's Day and, with some exceptions, not on the Sabbath any longer. Prayers were

[2] Cf. Oscar Cullmann, *Early Christian Worship* (Naperville, Ill: Alec R. Allenson, 1953); and *The Earliest Christian Confessions* (London: Lutterworth Press, 1949).

surely offered outside the hour of corporate worship, as well as
during the worship, and the same was probably true for hymns,
benedictions, creeds, collections of money, and the breaking of
bread. It is extremely difficult to assert that this or that action
could only have taken place within a corporate service, especially
since it is merely a matter of definition whether we would like
to call a missionary address (e.g., Acts 2:14-36; 3:12-26; 5:21)
a "worship service." It would probably be better not to confuse
an evangelistic sermon with the regular assembly of the faithful,
and the same will be true with regard to baptismal instructions
or specific meetings for the purpose of teaching. Even if we leave
out those occasions, we cannot say which actions and functions
were *necessary* for a corporate worship. Oscar Cullmann's
thesis,[3] which had been posed earlier by Adolf Deissmann, that
the Lord's Supper belonged to each worship service is not accepted without dispute. Even if it seems clear that we should
make a distinction between missionary preaching and meetings
for instruction on the one hand and the worship services on the
other hand, it would not be wise to go further to distinguish
between various types of worship in one local church. The texts
do not support these differentiations. It seems to be equally
clear that there was a great variety of forms of worship, when
we compare one church with another. There were various
streams of traditions, and it would seem feasible to recognize a
form of worship influenced by the early beginnings in Jerusalem,
and another form which was roughly common to the Pauline
churches. But all systematizing is impossible, since the Jewish-
Christian, as well as the Pauline churches, had incorporated
parts of Jewish traditions, as the doxologies and hymns seem
to show.[4] It is not meaningful to try to trace back forms of early
Christian worship to the Temple service as the root of the
Lord's Supper, and to the synagogue service as the origin of
preaching sermons. The influence of the synagogue on the early

[3] *Early Christian Worship,* pp. 26-36.
[4] Cf. Samuel L. Terrien, *The Hebraic Roots of Christian Worship,* the
1954 Reinecker Lectures, a private publication.

worship of the Christians has long been overestimated.[5] It is even questionable whether more knowledge of the historical influences on the early worship would really help us to understand the meaning of Christian worship. There were certainly great differences between the forms of worship in the younger Churches, and it even seems careless to talk about a "Pauline" type of church or form of worship (e.g., it would not be wise to generalize the results of the exegesis of 1 Corinthians 11, 12, and 14, and to apply them to all the Pauline churches).

After having approached the texts with this second question concerning the actual parts of the worship services, we come to the conclusion that the New Testament does not provide answers which could be utilized directly for our own understanding of worship. We must therefore ask a third question: What was the meaning of a worship service? Why did the early Christians gather for corporate worship? Only when we find an answer to this question, can we proceed to our main question concerning the sermon as part of our Sunday service.

Our first two questions, concerning possible names and actual parts of worship, were restricted to linguistic and historical investigations. Many detailed studies have been carried out in this field, and it is difficult to summarize or harmonize the results of modern scholarship. Even if we assumed that we could reach a general agreement on the exegesis of the passages dealing with worship, so that we could define precisely what the early Christian worship was, one question would still be left, namely: Should we in our worship copy the early Christians? Should we worship according to a pattern which might be discovered in the New Testament? An affirmative answer would actually imply that the outward forms and parts of worship are the things that really matter, and that the worship is to be understood as the

[5] Cf. "Die Lesungen," a new examination of the question by Gerhard Kunze in *Leiturgia*, K. F. Müller and W. Blankenburg, editors (Kassel: Stauda-Verlag, 1955), Vol. II, pp. 87-179. The three volumes of *Leiturgia* offer an enormous amount of material that should be known by all who study seriously in the field of worship.

work, effort, and creation of man. The validity or "orthodoxy" of a worship service would then depend upon how faithfully the early Christian worship is copied and imitated. This conception ignores the incarnation, ministry, death, and resurrection of Jesus Christ, and the Holy Spirit would be dealt with as an object of our liturgical thoughts. Since the worship service is the work, effort, and creation of Jesus Christ through the Holy Spirit, we must ask our question from that angle. The subject who acts in the worship service is the risen Lord, and it is He who forms the believers into one body with Himself through the Holy Spirit.

The meaning of the worship service and the reason for the gathering of the worshipers is to be sought in the work of Jesus Christ Himself. He holds the office of proclamation, and it is the Holy Spirit in whom the Church lives and gathers, and through whom the crucified, risen, and exalted Christ makes Himself known. What are the textual evidences for this statement?

It is not without significance that the "first day of the week," the Lord's day, had priority over other days for the meetings of the believers for corporate worship. (Acts 20:7; 1 Corinthians 16:2; Didache 14:1; Justin *Apology* I, 67: 3; etc.) Against the background of the Jewish week, the term "first day of the week" must be understood as the day after the Sabbath. It is not out of the question to speculate that the early Christians could have chosen Friday as the "main" day for their worship services. But they did not do this, and there is no doubt whatever that Sunday derives its importance from the Easter day. Sunday with its echo of Easter is the day of the risen Lord, and the worship on that day is distinct from that of the other days of the week, insofar as Sunday was thought to be appropriate for the assembly of the believers who are under the power of the victorious Lord. The "coming together" of the believers as the *ekklesia* happens in the Spirit; they "worship God in spirit, and glory in Christ Jesus" (Philippians 3:3), because "those who worship him must worship in spirit and truth" (John 4:24). The whole worship is *en pneumati*, in the Spirit. (1 Corinthians 12:3.) The body of Christ is being formed during the hour of worship through the Spirit. The believers bow down under the Word of grace and judgment and humiliate themselves under the Lord and under one another. In this way they "glory in Christ" and "boast" in Him. All the passages which speak of "edification" must be understood in this sense. The body of Christ takes shape, and the "building up" (1 Corinthians 14; Ephesians 4) involves the whole congregation. Each member (Romans 15:2) edifies his brother in "mutual upbuilding" (Romans 14:19), so that in Jesus Christ, the chief cornerstone, "the whole structure is joined together and grows into a holy temple in the Lord" (Ephesians 2:21). All the "grace gifts" were given "for building up the body of Christ" (Ephesians 4:12). However, the term "building up," which is in many ways better than the ambiguous term "edification," must not be misunderstood as if the members of the Church were growing and climbing higher and higher, until they reached the Head of the Church. The Church is being built up "downward," so to speak, from Jesus Christ "from whom the whole body, joined and knit together by every joint with which it is supplied, when each part is working properly, makes bodily growth and upbuilds itself in love." (Ephesians 4:16.) Jesus Christ is not "represented" by one or several men, e.g., by the "clergy," when the work of upbuilding takes place, but all the members take an active part in the service. The power and presence of the risen and ascended Lord is made manifest in the "grace gifts." The passage 1 Corinthians 11:18 indicates that the voices of all the people could be heard during the worship: "when you assemble as a church, I hear that there are divisions among you." Just the opposite is true with us. Our lack of unity would not be obvious during our worship, because only one or two people will be heard, and their words will be well prepared to avoid collisions and complications. At least at Corinth, it seems that the early worship was actively performed by all the members: "if all prophesy, and an unbeliever or outsider enters, he is convicted by all, he is called to account by all" and he will fall on his face and worship God and confess "that God is really among you." (1 Corinthians 14:24-25.) Compared with our modern form of worship, this sounds very strange! All members are actors on the stage. No one belongs passively to the audience, but if a passive spectator should accidentally enter he would immediately be made an active participant. How could this be possible in our large city churches?

In conclusion, we can say that the New Testament is extremely reluctant to provide concrete answers to the questions about the form and the parts of the worship service of the early Christians. Constitutive for a worship service is the assembly of believers, and it is the exalted Christ who works through the Holy Spirit, and who forms the believers into His own body. Inasmuch as the death and resurrection of Christ is for all people, it is the totality of the people in the Church who participate actively with their "grace gifts" during the hour of worship. There is no auditorium, for they are all on the stage. This was technically possible, since it seems that the congregations were small in numerical size. After daily services in the earliest time (Acts 2:46; 5:42), the fact that Sunday became the proper day for worship points to Easter Sunday and the risen Lord. It should not, therefore, be impossible to make a relative distinction between the hour of worship and the service in general during the week (*latreia, thysia, leiturgia,* etc.). That is, the believers participate in the servanthood of Christ who is present in their service during the week, but they anticipate their perfect union with the coming Lord, the exalted Christ, during the hour of worship. This thesis, however, must be examined later.

2. THE READING AND PREACHING OF THE BIBLICAL WORD

The early Christians did not have regular Scripture readings of the canonical Bible in their worship services. The Reformers, likewise, did not practice Scripture reading in addition to the sermon. The "liturgy" and Scripture reading are not more objec-

tive than the sermon. The written Word demands the spoken proclamation. The worship service does not reflect upon the "history of salvation" but is in itself part of it. The hour of worship is not a "drama," but the time of the real presence of the Servant Lord, who serves and calls His people. His serving is prior to man's serving.

According to the New Testament, the real presence of Jesus Christ is intimately connected with the Word. The doctrine of the three forms of the Word of God expresses faithfully the fact that the proclaimed Word is not merely an interpretation or repetition of, or a meditation upon the "real" Word, but that it is itself the real and true Word of God. The disciples are commissioned to go out and to preach the Word. They do not spread an idea, which can be accepted or rejected just as people please, but their preaching is the visitation of Jesus Christ Himself: "And if the house is worthy, let your peace come upon it; but if it is not worthy, let your peace return to you. . . . Truly, I say to you, it shall be more tolerable on the day of judgment for the land of Sodom and Gomorrah than for that town." (Matthew 10:13, 15.) "He who hears you hears me, and he who rejects you rejects me." (Luke 10:16.) This commission is not only "valid" for the time prior to Crucifixion or Easter, as if Christ could only be present in the words of His disciples during His earthly ministry, but the same charge is given after the Resurrection and is related to the receiving of the Holy Spirit: " 'Peace be with you. As the Father has sent me, even so I send you.' And when he had said this, he breathed on them, and said to them, 'Receive the Holy Spirit. If you forgive the sins of any, they are forgiven; if you retain the sins of any, they are retained.' " (John 20:21-23.) What does this mean for the worship service?

The passages of the commission, quoted from the Gospels, cannot directly be applied to the worship service of the early Christians. Nevertheless, it is quite obvious that the proclamation of the Word was the central part of the early worship

services. Preaching, prophesying, and teaching are all connected
with the Word. We must distinguish, however, between preaching or prophesying in the form of short, unprepared, and radical
appeals, on the one hand, and, on the other hand, teaching as an
instruction, exposition, or exhortation to a certain group of
people who come together regularly for meetings. This distinction has often been overemphasized, and it has become cus-
tomary to label it with the terms *kerygma* and *didache*. We will
see later that this terminology is only of limited value. In any
case, it is the Word in which the exalted Christ speaks to the
assembled believers, who are incorporated into one body with
Christ through the Holy Spirit. The question now arises as to
which form of the Word it is that makes the presence of Christ
manifest. Is it the Scripture reading or the sermon, or both?

There is not much support in the New Testament for those
who maintain that the Scripture readings in our services are
more "valid" and authoritative than the sermon. In line with
the pattern of the synagogue and the Qumran community, the
early Christians could have introduced the Scripture reading
into their worship services, but they did not do it. The Qumran
community practiced the reading and interpretation of the Law
"at any time of day or night." "The general members of the
community are to keep awake for a third of all the nights of
the year reading book(s), studying the Law and worshiping
together."[6] And the orthodox Jews, of course, had their regular
Scripture reading in the synagogue services according to a plan
of lessons. It has been taken for granted for a long time by New
Testament scholars that the early Christians had formed their
worship under the influence of the synagogue. This conception,
however, cannot be proved, in spite of the striking similarities
between the synagogue and the Early Church.[7] An influence

[6] Manual of Discipline translated by T. H. Gaster, *The Dead Sea Scriptures* (Garden City, N. Y.: Doubleday & Company, Inc., 1956), pp. 49-50.
[7] Both the synagogue and the early *basilica* were often divided into three
parts by columns; both had balconies for women, special rooms for baptismal purposes, and were oriented to the East; prayer, benediction, and
preaching were to be found in both.

of the synagogue cannot be shown before the year 150, when
Justin writes that "the memoirs of the apostles or the writings
of the prophets are read aloud as long as time permits."[8] Nor is
it any wonder that the early Christians did not adopt the order
of worship of the synagogue, since the gentile churches were
opposed to the theology of the synagogue, and they would hardly
have adopted the most important part of its life, namely its order
of worship.[9] However, there are some exceptions, such as a
hidden reference to a "reader" in Mark 13:14 and Matthew 24:15;
and the Revelation also says, "Blessed is he who reads aloud the
words of the prophecy, and blessed are those who hear." (1:3.)
The strongest passage is surely 1 Timothy 4:13, "Till I come,
attend to the public reading of scripture, to preaching, to teaching." However, the translation of the Revised Standard Version is
really misleading, because the whole phrase "to the public reading of scripture" is a rather free translation of the single Greek
word *te anagnosei*. The Epistles were no doubt read to all the
members of the church, and it seems that this was done during
the hour of corporate worship, because many closing benedictions of the Epistles were also opening salutations for the Eucharist. Perhaps, then, the Lord's Supper was celebrated after
the reading of the apostolic Epistle. There are no clear references to public readings of Old Testament lessons, and only the
Old Testament was the canonical "Bible," which alone would
interest us in this context.[10]

Not before the end of the second century do we find evidence
for a closer connection between the form of worship of the
synagogue and that of the Church. Only later is the Church
equipped with a formal "lectionary," i.e., with a list of passages

[8] *Apology* I, 67.

[9] This is indicated by the fact that the early Christian worship centered
around the prophetic and kerygmatic proclamation and the Lord's Supper
(however seriously one would take Cullmann's thesis), whereas these elements were absent in the synagogue, which emphasized teaching.

[10] 1 Corinthians 4:6 says, "that you may learn by us to live according to
scripture," which does not refer to public reading but rather to a (gnostic?)
heresy which wants to abolish the use of the Old Testament.

of the Old and New Testaments appropriate for each Sunday
in the "Christian Year." Only on that basis could the Church
assume that fixed readings and formulated prayers were the
necessary criteria for a "valid" Church service. Along with this
came the stress upon the mechanical understanding of the Lord's
Supper as a sacrament which works *ex opere operato,* and the
importance of a consecrated altar and church building, which
was — and in the Roman Church still is — necessary for proper
worship. The ordination of the priest, the consecration of the
altar with the elements of the Supper, and the automatic "holi-
ness" of the Bible became infinitely more important than the
proclamation of the Word. We have to examine our own understanding of worship very carefully, lest we adopt parts of a
tradition which is not based on the Biblical witness.[11] It is surprising to see that the Reformers, who did not possess our tools
of historical research, thought about the worship service as if
they knew that the early Christians had not practiced regular
Scripture reading. Calvin and Bullinger did not have a Scripture reading in addition to the sermon. The early Luther was
also skeptical about it, and the introduction to his Deutsche
Messe of 1526[12] speaks of the "young and ignorant people," who
might be improved in their knowledge of the Bible[13] and have
an increasing love for the Biblical Word, the "liturgical parts"
of the service thus having pedagogical value![14] This understanding of the extreme importance of the spoken word over against
the reading of the Word is even more interesting when we
realize that the Reformers were by no means influenced by one
and the same tradition. On the contrary, while Zwingli and the
South German Lutherans were influenced by the tradition of
preaching services by the friars in the centuries before the

---

[11] Cf. the very helpful and constructive elaborations by David H. C. Read,
"The Reformation of Worship," *Scottish Journal of Theology,* Vol. VII,
No. 4; Vol. VIII, No. 1 and No. 3 (1954-55).

[12] *Weimarer Ausgabe,* 19, pp. 72 ff.

[13] *Ibid.,* p. 73.

[14] However, the fact that Luther also introduced the chanting of the
lesson indicates that he was inclined to think of it as something "objective"!

Reformation, Luther and Calvin had no concrete knowledge of these fortunate, but rather local traditions, and elaborated their understanding of the worship service by re-examining the elements of the Roman Mass. Nevertheless, in spite of the different backgrounds, they reached the same result. The preached Word cannot be superseded by liturgical formulas, or even by the recital of the written Word of the Bible. The Reformers understood that the second form of the Word of God is dead if it does not break through to the first form. God has "qualified us to be ministers of a new covenant, not in a written code but in the Spirit; for the written code kills, but the Spirit gives life." (2 Corinthians 3:6.) The Church lives in the Spirit, who personally involves the participants in the office of proclamation. No one is allowed to hide behind the witness of others. The witness of the prophets and apostles demands a new witness, the prophet or apostle through whom the Holy Spirit witnesses to the presence of the risen Lord.

The decisive importance of the presence of Jesus Christ in the worship service can be illustrated by an examination of the misunderstanding of worship in the Eastern Orthodox Church. Although the Orthodox Church is, in many ways, far ahead of us with regard to the seriousness of prayer, adoration, and discipline in humiliation, it has to be said that its understanding of worship is rather like a "drama," which repeats and portrays the divine history. The history of God with His people is described from the Creation to the Fall; from there to the giving of the Law; to the prophets and the Incarnation, covering the ministry, death, and resurrection of the Lord; and leading up to the promised fulfillment at the day of the second Advent. All this is "performed," so that the congregation can observe, admire, and adore what happens on the "stage" of the church, which is the altar space in the Roman Church or the picture wall in the Orthodox Church. The complete "Christian Drama" is reproduced and portrayed. It would be very one-sided to say that this is the case only in the Orthodox Church or in the Roman Church, for it is unfortunately also the conception of many in the Protes-

tant Churches. Many of our sermons are nothing more than an
attempt to reproduce and illustrate in a dramatic way what God
has done and what He will do, while many of our hymns are
more reproductive and imitative than are the Eastern icons.
The Scripture reading, above all, is the clearest expression of
conceiving the worship service as an impersonal re-enactment
of God's acts, especially when the ridiculous demand is made
that the Church members place themselves in the position of
the "men and women of the Bible." Later we will try to say why
it is not only impossible but unbiblical to persuade church members to believe that they "are" Abraham, Isaiah, Martha, or
Peter.[15] D. T. Niles expresses it convincingly when he compares
the Hindu doctrine of reincarnation with the incarnation of the
Lord. "If reincarnation is true, then persons are only 'dramatis
personae.' The acts and scenes change and the same people play
different roles dressed differently for different parts. The drama
has meaning while it lasts, but when it ends only the actors are
left, each a separate individual, their relationship to one another on the stage having no permanent significance."[16] A worship service can never be a parable of a "truth" which lies behind it. It is neither a drama, nor a melodrama, nor an "opera,"
as it might seem to be in many churches; but it is a *scene* in the
drama of the history of God with His people. There cannot be
spectators who adore what is being performed, there can only
be participants, whose adoration is their complete participation
in the work of mutual edification. Each service is a new act of
God, or else it is not a service. The time of God's speaking is a
unique and unrepeatable time. This is what Martin Buber means
by "Faktumseinzigkeit" (the uniqueness of the fact). The Word
itself is on its way: it creates, judges, and gives life; it challenges,
comforts, and heals. It is God Himself who has the initiative,
and who offers, commands, and demands. And it is also God
Himself in the Holy Spirit, who "is at work in you, both to will
and to work for his good pleasure." (Philippians 2:13.) Chris-

[15] Cf. pp. 160-161.
[16] *The Preacher's Task and the Stone of Stumbling,* p. 33.

tian worship is, therefore, radically different from all religious sacrifices and services, for in Christian worship it is the Holy Spirit who is both commanding and obeying. God not only confronts the Church, but He is also at work in the Church; He is on the side of the believers, working on their behalf and standing in their place. Man does not know how to worship or how to approach the Creator of heaven and earth unless God Himself enables him to believe and to respond. "For we do not know how to pray as we ought, but the Spirit himself intercedes for us." (Romans 8:26.) We must, therefore, question the propriety of the term "divine worship," or even "worship." The New Testament, as we have seen, does not employ a special term for the hour of corporate worship. In itself that would not be a reason against our using such a term. However, the term "divine worship" grew out of the medieval understanding of worship and should be used with care. The first definition of "worship" cannot be that people "do something" with God, or offer something, or themselves, to God. The first statement about worship must be, under all circumstances, that it is God who does something with His people. It is legitimate to say that *God serves* His people during the hour of worship. Inseparably connected with this is man's service toward God. We could not speak of the latter without first accepting the former. "For the Son of man also came not to be served but to serve, and to give his life as a ransom for many" (Mark 10:45; compare Matthew 20:28); "I am among you as one who serves" (Luke 22:27). These words, as well as the washing of the feet in John 13, cannot be understood when they are taken out of context: those who are being served by Christ are immediately called into His service. They serve Him by serving one another. Nevertheless, God's serving is prior to man's serving, just as His love comes to us before our love is possible.

One can debate these interpretations and perhaps formulate the results in a different way. But there is no doubt, nor can it be debated, that the hour of corporate worship is a part of the history of God with His people, and not an hour of instruction

or meditation upon that history. This is definitely the understanding of the New Testament. The risen Christ proclaims
Himself through the Holy Spirit, who makes faith, understanding, prayer, and preaching possible. Biblically and dogmatically
it is quite impossible to make a distinction between the sermon
and the "liturgy" by saying that the latter is more "objective,"
or that it represents the presence of Christ more purely. Least
of all can one say that the Scripture reading is "safer" than the
sermon. The written witness of the Biblical books must again
become spoken witness: proclamation. Rather than being the
result of didactical or methodological thinking, it is the will of
Christ Himself that His Word be preached by His servants who
are called to be His witnesses. He speaks through their mouths.
Otherwise, it would be desirable to invite the congregation to
come together in the church to listen to a tape recording of
Scripture lessons read by an expert in elocution, and to claim
that this reading were the ideal form of pure proclamation.[17]

In summary: the early Christians were probably not influenced by the synagogue and had no Scripture reading of the
canonical Bible. It is also a fact that no consecrated buildings,
altars, and persons were regarded as criteria for a true service.
The assembled people are the temple and the sanctuary. There
is no division between the actors and the audience. The present
Christ acts in the Holy Spirit, so that the believers are formed
into one body with Him. The service, therefore, does not reflect
upon the "history of salvation," but is in itself part of it. The
hour of worship is neither a drama nor an opera on the theme
"God's mighty acts in history"; rather it is the time of the real
presence of the Servant Lord, who serves and calls into His
service His people. This Biblical understanding was rediscovered
by the Reformers, in spite of the various traditions of worship
by which they were influenced. This result enables us to come
to some practical suggestions, which now have to be elaborated.

[17] It is rather ironical that one would sometimes prefer this kind of service
to a poor sermon!

3. SCRIPTURE READING AND TEACHING

The Scripture reading and the interpretation of it must be understood as teaching. Preaching and teaching are intimately interwoven. But there is a definite priority of preaching over teaching, which corresponds to the priority of God's calling over man's understanding. The promise of the presence and self-revelation of Christ is given with regard to the sermon, but it is not confined to it. The Scripture reading in connection with a short teaching sermon, in addition to the proper sermon, has its legitimate, although not necessary, place in the worship service of the Church.

Logically, only two directions of speaking are possible during the hour of worship: the Word of God to man, and the words of man to God. However, Jesus Christ as true God and true man compels us to see that the Word of God comes to us through the writing and speaking of men, and that the speaking of man to God is possible only because of the obedience of the man Jesus Christ, in whose name we can pray and come to the Father.

Theoretically speaking, there is only room in the worship service for proclamation and prayer as the two basic elements. The sermon, many hymns, and the benediction can come under the category of "proclamation." The prayers, certain hymns, and the collection of money could belong to the category of "prayer." This view cannot be denied on grounds of Scriptures, and it leaves the door wide open for many other forms of worship. But it raises one question: Where does the Scripture reading belong?

Zwingli, the early Luther, Calvin, and Bullinger solve the problem by leaving out the "naked" Scripture reading altogether. Scripture must be interpreted by a living, human witness, or else it cannot be read. The Reformers introduced, therefore, the short "teaching sermon," before or after the Scripture reading. This short explanation or interpretation was given in addition to the ordinary sermon. These teaching sermons were often based on parts of catechisms, not necessarily on Scripture passages, which indicates quite clearly that the Scripture reading was seen by them in relation to teaching and instruction. Is there room for teaching in the hour of corporate worship?

We cannot find out with certainty whether or not the early Christians combined proclamation and teaching within one meeting. It is, therefore, probably necessary to think pragmatically and to join the Reformers by saying that there can be an element of teaching in the Sunday service, because our church members badly need more knowledge of the Bible. We can add that these minutes of teaching serve to increase the understanding of the sermon proper and help to strengthen all the people present to participate in the service.

We must again consider the possibility of a "naked" Scripture reading. Can it really never be proclamation, but always only teaching? It is not possible to systematize the answer. John Wesley's "Aldersgate experience," was caused by a Bible passage, or even a comment by Luther on a Bible verse, and not by a sermon. It is indeed possible that a Scripture reading, read in a specific situation, e.g., in a persecuted church, can be very powerful. Shortly after the war, I saw a completely destroyed city, and in the midst of it a wall of a former church building with an inscription in big capitals, saying: "Blessed are those who mourn, for they shall be comforted." These "uninterpreted" passages can at times interpret themselves, more so than the words of Isaiah 53, which were read by the Ethiopian (in Acts 8), who could not understand them "unless someone guides me" (8:31). Those who have already heard the Good News can hear the power of a simple quotation, which is also possible with the Scripture reading during the worship. The simple fact that it is just *this* man, who reads just *this* passage, in *this* situation, can be a witness in itself. The way in which a passage is read can be the beginning of proclamation.[18] Although the reader can

[18] Cf. Dietrich Bonhoeffer, *Life Together* (New York: Harper & Brothers, 1954), pp. 50 ff., especially p. 56.

destroy the prophetic or apostolic witness, he can also read it so that the first form of the Word of God (the proclaimed Word which is still hidden) is already present. Realistically we must admit how often we "have forgotten the Scripture reading" of a service. All preachers know how much time can be wasted when one tries to find a suitable Scripture reading to balance the sermon text! How many people really understand our secret theological thoughts and calculations, which made us select just this and not another Scripture reading?

Ordinarily the Scripture reading is only useful for didactic reasons, i.e., for knowledge of the Bible, as a substitute for weekday services and private Bible reading within the homes. The Reformers were realistic enough to look at the problem in that way. When there is the possibility of preaching a sermon, i.e., when the congregation is assembled, we should not refer to personal experiences of the power of this or that Bible quotation (as in the examples above), in order to say that Scripture reading should be used in addition to the sermon. This reasoning would imply that we do not trust the power of the proclaimed Word, but that we desire to have something more. In all honesty we should feel free to say that the Scripture reading most likely serves nothing more than a didactic purpose. For this reason, however, the Scripture reading should not be abolished, but rather it should be connected with a short teaching "sermon," which lasts not more than three to five minutes. Historical remarks, critical textual references, and explanations of important Biblical words are often artificial or embarrassing during a sermon. This necessary information can easily be made part of the Sunday service, when it is connected with the Scripture reading. The information is not primarily important for the sermon text and the sermon, but it simply helps to educate the church members to listen carefully and with more understanding to the Biblical word. The *lectio continua,* the reading of a whole Epistle or book of a prophet, over a period of many Sundays can be very helpful.

These statements are, in a way, a confession of the merely

pedagogical and didactic usefulness of the Scripture reading.
There is no theological necessity for it to belong to the regular
corporate worship, but neither is there a reason against it. The
time of weekday services, with teaching sermons, is in most
countries passé. It is therefore almost necessary to use the hour
on Sunday morning as wisely as possible, so that the teaching
is not merely confined to the Sunday school, which only very
seldom reaches all the people who are willing "to go to church"
on Sunday. Even if all the members of a church were present at
the special teaching hour before the actual worship, there is the
danger that the Sunday school (for very human and personal
reasons) could become a separate church, distinct from worshiping community. The responsible members would also be badly
divided, so that the "teachers" are responsible for the teaching
hour, and the "preacher," isolated from them, for the preaching
hour.

C. H. Dodd's distinction of teaching and preaching (in the
year 1936, but — in this form — later withdrawn by him) is justified within limits. But it would be impossible to systematize the
distinction between *kerygma* and *didache* by saying that Christ
in His presence uses only the preaching to make Himself known,
while the teaching is only the word of man; or by saying that
preaching and teaching start at different points but work toward
the same goal, namely the building up of the church. The first
definition is one-sided because Christ, in His self-revelation, is
not restricted to the sermonic word of man, nor is He forced by
the sermon to reveal Himself. The second definition is false,
because preaching and teaching have the same point of departure, namely God's self-disclosure in Jesus Christ, although their
goals are different. We do not try to "achieve" one and the same
end when teaching in a theological seminary or in a Sunday
school, and when preaching in a worship service. The goals are
different, but the reason that we do it and the source from which
our words come is the same. There cannot be an absolute distinction between preaching and teaching, because the living
Word is free to be present, not only in the sermon but also in

the words of teaching. Likewise, a sermon may convey more instruction and information than the preacher intended. The distinction between the two is relative; the living Word is not confined to the distinction, but man should pay attention to it. Preaching and teaching, as two functions, are interwoven, so that either of them in isolation would be untrue. Preaching without teaching would be like a skeleton without flesh, and teaching without preaching would be like a body without bones. A church without teaching does not know history and has no history; it is like a call without an answer. A church that only teaches has no present and no future; it is like an answer without the call. All this can be observed in the Biblical texts, where preaching is often transformed into teaching, and where teaching can again lead to preaching: for example, the transformation of preaching into teaching in the New Testament Epistles, which were to a large extent originally sermons; and the transformation of teaching into preaching in Deuteronomy, which seems to be the preaching of the Levitical reform movement, in which the teaching tradition was recast into sermonic form. We will later try to uncover the relative distinction between preaching and teaching, as analogous to the distinction between the Word and the sacraments, the sermon and the liturgy, and the "office bearers" and the congregation.

Preaching and teaching are intimately interwoven. Nevertheless, there is a definite priority of preaching over teaching, which corresponds to the priority of God's calling over man's understanding. Since the hour of corporate worship is the time of the real presence of the exalted Lord in the assembly of the believers through the Holy Spirit, we must say that the self-revelation of Jesus Christ and the humiliation of the people under His Word is what constitutes the service. In this way we come back to our previous conclusion that teaching is not a genuine part of the worship service as such, but there are no reasons against having a Scripture reading connected with a short teaching sermon during the hour of worship. The Scripture reading and the explanation of it can be called a "school for the understanding of the sermon." In the same way the responsive reading of the psalms can be called a "school of prayer." Neither of them is necessarily "real" proclamation or "real" prayer, but they *serve* the sermon and the prayer.[19]

There are many interesting attempts to introduce new types of "teaching services" on weekdays, especially in Holland. An experienced preacher, or a group of specially trained preachers, is responsible for regular and public teaching sermons within a city. They work on behalf of the local churches. These meetings are not intended to be "worship services," in the strict sense of the word; they are rather open evangelistic gatherings with a special emphasis on teaching and instruction. Questions of dogmatics, the Bible, and the history of the Church are dealt with, as well as current issues of the life in the Church and the world, e.g., marriage, family, education, politics, economics, etc. It is apparent, however, that these experiments could also lead to a split between the local congregations and a special audience of a favorite intercongregational teaching preacher.

A compromise between these evening "teaching services" and the normal Sunday service without teaching would be the short teaching sermon during the hour of the public service in the local church. Surely one cannot argue against it by saying that a teaching sermon, in addition to the proper sermon, would ask too much of the patience of the church members. One or two long Scripture readings which are hard to understand are more tiring than five minutes of solid instruction. Many people will appreciate some brief dogmatical and Biblical information, even if it were only to avoid the constant repetition of well-known Scripture readings, like the 23rd or 90th Psalm, or 1 Corinthians 13. It would seem that preachers frequently underestimate the intellectual ability and hunger of the ordinary church members, by using only well-known words and passages or — what is

[19] It should be noticed that very few of the psalms are real prayers. The elements of teaching, creed, law, and proclamation are contained in many psalms, so that not only God is addressed but also man. A passage of a psalm which addresses man cannot be a prayer.

worse — by believing that unintelligible words of the Bible would explain themselves mystically because they are words of the Bible! One ought to look realistically at the lack of the knowledge of the Bible and to consider at the same time the honest desire of many church members to know more about the Bible and the teaching of the Church.

In summary it can be said that teaching differs from preaching by proceeding according to the order 3-2-1 of the three forms of the Word of God,[20] and one can even go a step further to say that the difference between teaching and preaching corresponds to the difference between the witness *(martys)* and the herald *(keryx)*, although these terms should not be too sharply distinguished. Perhaps it is most appropriate to conceive of the Scripture reading as teaching, although one must realize that it cannot be said that the voice of the living Lord could not break through when a Bible passage is being read and interpreted in a didactic manner. According to the promise, however, the Church must expectantly await the presence and self-revelation of its Lord in the sermon, and not in the words of instruction. But one cannot systematize this statement, as if Christ were confined to the sermon. The Scripture reading in connection with a short teaching sermon can at least serve to lead to better understanding of the sermon and the daily life in the Church. It has its legitimate, although not necessary, place in the worship service of the Church.

4. THE PRAYER AND THE LORD'S SUPPER
IN RELATION TO THE PROCLAMATION

The distinction between "visible" and "invisible" Words of God is unfortunate. The sacraments are not the objectification of the sermon, because the exalted Christ is not present in two different ways. The relative distinction between adoration and proclamation must be seen in the light of the union with Christ,

[20] Cf. pp. 42-44.

because of whom the sermon is ultimately adoration, and the prayer and the adoration ultimately an offer from God. The sermon and the Lord's Supper are not "contra-distinguished," but it is the one life-giving Word that is present in both. The presence of the risen Lord and the expectation of His return are the decisive elements in the sermon and the Lord's Supper; we bear in mind both when we say "proclamation."

The sacraments, as distinct from the sermon, are often said to belong to the "liturgy" of the worship service and not to the proclamation. The sacraments are thus seen to be related to "adoration" rather than to the sermon. This false alternative is very misleading. The sacraments are not "over against" the Word of the sermon, nor are they "visible words," as distinct from the Word of the sermon. This Augustinian distinction is unfortunate, for it implies that the Word of the sermon is "invisible." The Bible does not make a case for the difference between visible and invisible. The sacraments are not a substitute for the Word, nor are they the objectification or perfection of the Word. The exalted Christ is not present in two different ways, i.e., in a sermonic and in a sacramental way. It is not even sufficient to say that the sacraments "belong" to the sermon, or that the sermon is necessary for the sacraments, but rather that both, the sermon and the sacraments, are proclamation. Certainly there is a distinction between the two, but it is not the distinction of liturgy-proclamation, or adoration-sermon.

Before this question is pursued further, it might be appropriate to inquire whether there is a part of the worship which is clearly distinct from proclamation. It seems that prayer is to be sharply distinguished from proclamation, thus constituting a partition of worship. We return here to our basic problem of the first chapter: the question of the word of man to God in relation to the Word of God to man. These two parts are necessary elements of worship, and it seems that the various "parts" of the worship service can be related either to the category of prayer or to the category of proclamation. It has already been

shown that the term "adoration" cannot be used here very meaningfully, since adoration embraces much more than prayer; not
only prayer and the worship service are adoration, but also the
total activity of Christians is adoration, including *leitourgia*
(liturgy). It does not make sense to speak of "adoration" or
"liturgy" as an alternative to proclamation.

Prayer and proclamation, however, might appear to be two
categories or alternatives which cannot be equated. The two
might be conceived to be so different in "essence" that it would
be impossible to overcome this "dualism." Indeed, proclamation
is directed toward people, while prayer is strictly directed
toward God. Any softening or compromising of these basic
statements could not be tolerated. When the minister prays, he
speaks on behalf of all the believers present; he does not speak
to them. They all join his words and repeat the words within
themselves. No one other than God is listening. Prayers which
contain news, instructions, proclamations, little hints for the
members of the church, etc., are not really prayers.

This clear distinction must be understood in analogy to the
clear distinction between the word of the Church and the Word
of God to the Church. But the "Christological analogy" has made
it necessary to say that actually we cannot speak of an "un-
human, divine" Word of God to man, and an "undivine, human"
word of man to God. The living God is "over against" His people,
above and beyond them, so that they must look up to Him,
admire and adore (in the common understanding of the word)
Him. But He is also in Jesus Christ through the Holy Spirit
really present among them. He is in their place, commanding
and responding, demanding and obeying, preaching and praying. It has been said that the risen Lord is the true preacher
and His own Evangelist; that proclamation is the self-proclamation of Jesus Christ, and that to accept this fact is inevitable for
the proper understanding of preaching. Furthermore, these
things can be said in precisely the same way with regard to
prayer. Prayer is not man's effort, and it is therefore not his
work. If it were his work, one would fall back to a religious

understanding of Christian worship and would do better by going to school at a Buddhist temple, in order to learn how to be lifted up, to meditate, and to go beyond himself. Otherwise we have to go to the school of prayer in the psalms and other parts of the Bible, where we learn that it is Jesus Christ Himself who takes us into His prayer.

Christians do not pray in their own name, but in the name of Jesus Christ, which means recognizing the power which this name possesses. Prayer is the power of the Man Jesus, who is in solidarity with men, and who asks men to subdue themselves to His power. God answers the requests of men because they are summed up in Jesus Christ, and because it is Jesus Christ who prays.[21] The exalted Lord continues to pray as the heavenly Intercessor. God the Holy Spirit takes men into the prayer of Jesus Christ. While this is the work of the Holy Spirit, it does not mean that men remain passive. Prayer is an act on men's part, and as such it calls for his full participation, which is made possible, initiated, guided, and fulfilled by the Holy Spirit. We say exactly the same of preaching, which is also the self-revelation of Jesus Christ through the Holy Spirit, and as such it is His work; yet it is man's obligation to give his utmost and literally to risk his life with the living God.

While it is true to say that the sermon is the Word of God from the outside to the Church, it is equally true to say that the sermon is adoration because it is the work of Jesus Christ. He is the Mediator not only from God to man but also from man to God. Thus the sermon is not only preached "for our salvation" but also for the glory of God. God is not only made known in Jesus Christ; He is also glorified in Him. That He is made known is, in fact, glorification. Therefore, in precisely the same way, prayer is man's word to God, and it is equally true that the prayer is Jesus Christ's work through the Holy Spirit. "The Spirit himself intercedes for us with sighs too deep for words.

[21] All this has been expressed in a marvelous way by Dietrich Bonhoeffer in his little study on the Psalms, *Das Gebetbuch der Bibel* (Bad Salzuflen: MBK-Verlag, 1946).

. . . the Spirit intercedes for the saints according to the will of God." (Romans 8:26-27.) Without contradicting the first presuppositions, it is possible and necessary to say that proclamation is "offered" *to* God and that prayer is a gift *from* God. This is, of course, a conclusion and not the point of departure. The Biblical presupposition is that proclamation comes *from* God to man, and that prayer comes from man *to* God. It is only because of the hypostatic union that one can see how these two seemingly contradictary statements are one in Jesus Christ. On the basis of this Biblical doctrine, it can and must be said that the work of man for God cannot be separated from the work of God for man. "For God is at work in you, both to will and to work for his good pleasure." (Philippians 2:13.)[22]

The conclusion, then, is that prayer is only relatively different from preaching, as far as these two parts of the worship are conceived as two "categories." It is theologically not possible to speak of two ultimately different parts of the worship service. Praying and preaching must, however, be distinguished as far as our human intentions, preparations, and formulations are concerned. We do not preach or pray to God during the sermon; we speak to people and make this outwardly manifest by looking into their faces. On the other hand, we do not inform, instruct, or preach to people when we pray; we speak to God and make this outwardly manifest by not looking into the faces of the people who pray. For preparing and conducting a worship service it is essential not to confuse these entirely different ways of speaking and addressing. But it is one and the same Jesus Christ whose presence in the assembly of the

[22] The quoting of Philippians 2:13 is certainly not sufficient to support this important thought. The passage is only used as a summary and title for the whole doctrine of union with Christ; it is not our task to elaborate it in this context. Cf. Karl Barth, *Church Dogmatics,* Vol. IV, Part 1; Paul M. van Buren, *Christ in Our Place* (Grand Rapids: Wm. B. Eerdmans Publishing Company, 1957); and T. F. Torrance, *Royal Priesthood.* A new and very thorough elaboration of the whole complex of questions is offered by Claude Welch in *The Reality of the Church* (New York: Charles Scribner's Sons, 1958).

believers constitutes a service of worship. He is the only obedient and true Preacher and the only obedient and true Intercessor and High Priest. He speaks in the sermon through the
Holy Spirit, and through the Holy Spirit He takes man into His
own prayer. The worship service is His work. The work of the
minister and the people is participation in this work.

Ultimately everything in Biblical thinking is unipolar and not
dualistic. If the split between object and subject (and between
theory and practice) is not any longer valid or constitutive anywhere in the world, it is in the Church; and if this distinction
is abolished anywhere in the Church, it is in the worship service.

The presence of the risen Christ is constitutive of true worship and is the dominant factor for all thinking about worship.
There is no ultimate split between prayer and proclamation,
and one cannot be isolated from the other. If all this be accepted,
it should be possible to reach an understanding of worship and
to find a form and order for it. But everyone who proceeds to
this concrete work realizes that neither the Bible nor the Reformation provides definite prescriptions concerning the form and
order for worship. We will never find *the* form and order for
Christian worship, and the attempt to find it is childish. The
form and order do not control and command the presence of the
Risen Christ, but it is the Risen Christ who controls and dictates
the form and order. All efforts in local churches to "change the
liturgy" must, therefore, be done in obedience and love. Love is
the first command for those who attempt to change the order
of worship in their church.

In our considerations thus far, the Lord's Supper has not been
mentioned specifically. Without attempting to go into the exegetical and historical questions in detail, it will be necessary in
our context to examine the understanding of the Lord's Supper.
The necessity for thinking of the sermon *and* the Lord's Supper
together can be shown when we use the term "proclamation."
The presence of the risen Lord and the expectation of His return
are the decisive elements in both the sermon and the Lord's
Supper, and we bear these elements in mind when we say "pro-

clamation." The guiding question in the following investigation will therefore be this: What does the Biblical witness say about the Lord's Supper with regard to the presence of Christ and the anticipation of His return?

Basically, there are two different approaches to the question of the genesis of the Lord's Supper. One school[23] interprets the fundamental chapters (Mark 14 and 1 Corinthians 11) in the context of hellenistic syncretism; another school approaches the texts from the side of Jewish traditions, the Old Testament and the Biblical covenant as such. The latter school sees a parallel to the passover, although it will not always say that the Lord's Supper grew directly out of the Jewish passover.[24] There is no agreement between the two schools (or within them) as to whether Mark 14 and 1 Corinthians 11 are more than an Early Church liturgy; in other words, whether or not we can go "behind" these texts to prove that the words were spoken by Jesus, and not merely by the post-Easter community. Joachim Jeremias[25] finds aramaisms in the texts, thus proving that the origin of these earliest eucharistic liturgies cannot be hellenistic but must be palestinian. He concludes[26] from the fact that Jesus "interprets" the bread and the wine, that the Last Supper took place at the occasion of a passover meal, for it was typical at the passover for the father to "interpret" to the son the various parts of the celebration and the significance of the food. It is doubtful, however, whether one can agree with Jeremias that the "breaking of the bread" symbolizes the breaking of a body and the red wine the shedding of blood. K. G. Kuhn seems more convincing when he points out that there is a strong relation

[23] Peculiarly enough it is represented by New Testament scholars whose names end with "-mann": Bultmann, Käsemann, Conzelmann, Holtzmann, Deissmann, Lietzmann, and others—(but not Cullmann!)

[24] For a discussion of this point, see Theo Preiss, *Life in Christ* (Naperville, Ill.: Alec R. Allenson, Inc., 1954), pp. 81-99: "Was the Last Supper a Paschal Meal?"

[25] *The Eucharistic Words of Jesus* (New York: The Macmillan Company, 1955).

[26] Cf. the whole discussion with the careful statements and possible objections, *Ibid.*, pp. 14-60.

and influence between the communal meals of the Qumran Community and the early Christian Eucharist with its breaking of bread and blessing of the bread and the cup.[27] Jeremias and Kuhn agree, apparently, that the words concerning the cup and the bread were spoken by Jesus, but the two scholars give different reasons for it. This question is highly important because it is here that one has to make the decision whether "the words of institution" refer to the death of Christ or to the eschatological fulfillment of the promise of the heavenly meal with the Lord. Here, as well as in other places in the New Testament, the question whether or not we have the words of Jesus Himself (the *ipsissima vox Jesu*) in our texts, is not really of great concern. Far more important is whether or not we understand what the Biblical witnesses want us to know. Jeremias seems to be much too concerned with the *ipsissima vox* of Jesus,[28] and the last part of his conclusion leads to an interpretation of the Lord's Supper as a feast of His death.[29]

There is another way of approaching the problem. One can go backwards, so to speak, from the later liturgies of the Church to the sources of these liturgies. This was done some time ago by Hans Lietzmann,[30] who finds two main types: the ancient Egyptian liturgy, represented in a way by Serapion, and reaching back to the Didache; and the liturgy of Hippolytus. The former stresses clearly the eschatological conception of the Eucharist, the second advent of Christ, and the communion of the partakers of the meal. The latter emphasizes the death of Jesus Christ. Markus Barth[31] has shown that in the final analysis the

[27] Cf. K. G. Kuhn: "The Lord's Supper and the Communal Meal at Qumran," in *The Scrolls and the New Testament*, Krister Stendahl, editor (New York: Harper & Brothers, 1957), pp. 65-93.

[28] Cf. also the Foreword to his *The Parables of Jesus* (London: SCM Press, 1954).

[29] However, he too stresses the "eschatological looking forward"; cf. *The Eucharistic Words of Jesus*, pp. 115-118.

[30] *Messe und Herrenmahl, Eine Studie zur Geschichte der Liturgie* (Bonn, 1926).

[31] "Das Abendmahl, Passahmahl, Bundesmahl und Messiasmahl," *Theologische Studien*, 1945, Heft 18.

two conceptions are not mutually exclusive, and that the proper understanding of the Eucharist is grounded in the eschatological hope of fulfillment. The Eucharist is a meal, and the fulfillment will also be a meal.[32] Cullmann with good reasons denies the one-sided idea that the "breaking of bread" of the primitive community had nothing to do with the anticipation of the return of the Lord and the Messianic Banquet, and that 1 Corinthians 11 would be irreconilable with the other ancient traditions.[33] He stresses particularly the appearances of the risen Lord during the meals of the disciples. Both the joy which filled the hearts of the disciples and their anticipation of the return of the Lord determined their communal meals. The ancient prayer *Maranatha*, "Our Lord, come!", which is preserved in the Aramaic form, also indicates the expectation that the risen Lord will soon return for the Messianic Meal. Cullmann also points out the importance of Sunday as the "Lord's day" for the worship services. This importance further indicates that the Easter joy and the anticipation of the return of the Lord dominated in the worship service.

If the Lord's Supper took place at the occasion of a (passover) meal, shortly before the death of the Lord, and if the disciples gathered for the same meal shortly after Easter, then we can understand why Paul begins his account of what he has "received from the Lord" by saying: "the Lord Jesus on the night when he was betrayed . . ." Thus the passage in 1 Corinthians 11 by no means constitutes a break between two ideas about the Lord's Supper; rather it connects the two. The Lord's death is being proclaimed as often as they eat this bread and drink the cup, and it is only because of Easter and after Easter that His death is revealed in its full saving power. Easter reveals what has been accomplished by the Cross, and it is the "Easter" communion of the believers that proclaims His death,

[32] *Ibid.*, pp. 40 ff.
[33] *Early Christian Worship* (London: SCM Press, 1953); see also Oscar Cullmann and F. J. Leenhardt, *Essays on the Lord's Supper* (Richmond: John Knox Press, 1958), especially pp. 21-23.

which means that the reconciling glory of the Cross is made manifest. The Lord's Supper preaches how Easter day reveals the death of the Lord. We need not confine ourselves to 1 Corinthians 11, but we can examine all the Pauline passages which speak of the Lord's death in order to see that preaching the death means preaching the glory, the Resurrection, and the life at the same time. And this again, can only be preached in close connection with the coming glory: "you proclaim the Lord's death until he comes." (1 Corinthians 11:26.) This is the celebration of "the new Covenant." It is the risen Christ who is present among the partakers of the Communion; or better, He invites them to participate with Him in the meal at which His presence and His return in glory are being proclaimed. Those who eat with Him are on their way with open eyes and ears toward the eschatological fulfillment. We should free ourselves from the idea that the Lord's Supper is a memorial of His death, or, as it were, a repetition or a drama of His death. It is fair to say that a Biblical understanding of the Lord's Supper is possible without using the term or the idea of a "symbol." We do not eat Jesus Christ (that would be a symbol), but we eat with Him. We eat now with Him in this "last time" in our mortal life, and we shall eat with him anew at the wedding at the end of all times. There are innumerable passages in the Synoptics, in John, and in the Apocalypse describing salvation and fulfillment in terms of a wedding feast with the Lord as the bridegroom. These passages cannot be symbolized or spiritualized, as if the union with Christ were something better or something "beyond" the concrete communion with Him at one table. The participants at the Lord's Supper come from Easter, which revealed the fruits of the Cross, and they go to the end of all things with joy in their hearts. One must reject as exegetically impossible the idea that Christians meet at the Lord's table "to break together the bread of life," meaning that the body of Christ is broken again, as one sometimes hears. The body of the Lord was *not* "broken" as John 19:33 (cf. vs. 36) asserts, in fulfillment of Psalm 34:20, and in parallel to the prescriptions with regard to the paschal lamb in Exodus 12:46 and Numbers 9:12. The "breaking of bread" does not symbolize the death of Jesus Christ, or else one would have to symbolize the whole Lord's Supper, in order to avoid the false idea of a repetition of the death of Christ, as it is found in the Roman Mass. The words "This is my body which is for you" (1 Corinthians 11:24) indicate of course the relation of the Lord's Supper to Christ's death, but the fruits of His death can only be seen in the light of the victory of Easter and the hope of His return.

It seems possible to make two objections to this interpretation of the Lord's Supper as a proclamation of the present and the coming Lord. The first is the reference to the passover as a feast which was directed to an event in the past and not to the future. The second objection could come from an interpretation of the words of institution and the subsequent command: "This do in remembrance of me."

Concerning the first argument, it can very well be shown how much the feasts of Israel, especially the passover, contained a vivid element of eschatological hope.[34] The "recapitulation" of the events in the past is not a meditation or "remembrance" of the mighty act of God with the fathers, but rather a real solidarity with them caused by the presence of the living God who acts in the present and will act in the future. The German term *Vergegenwärtigung*[35] has to be introduced at this point; it will be used in the following chapter in the context of homiletics. It means a "making real and present" of acts in the past, which are also relevant for the future, a "recapitulative anticipation." It is in this sense that the passover is *Vergegenwärtigung* of the deliverance of God's people in the past. The liturgy of the pass-

[34] Cf. Walther Eichrodt, *Theologie des Alten Testaments* Vol. I, §11, (Berlin: Evangelische Verlagsanstalt, 1933, 1950); and Walther Zimmerli, "Verheissung und Erfüllung," *Evangelische Theologie,* 1952, 1/2, pp. 34-59.

[35] *Vergegenwärtigung* is the title of an important collection of essays by leading Old Testament scholars (Berlin: Evangelische Verlagsanstalt, 1955); it contains the articles of the well-known issue July/August 1952 of the *Evangelische Theologie,* and in addition essays by Rudolf Bultmann and by Claus Westermann. Cf. also my discussion below (pp. 145 ff.).

over looks back to the saving acts, makes them present, and directs the view toward the final redemption.[36] This "eschatological outlook" had its fixed place in the liturgy before the singing of the Hallel, Psalms 113-118. If, then, the Lord's Supper is the fulfillment of the passover as the feast of the new Covenant, it cannot be said that the influence of the passover upon the Lord's Supper makes impossible the interpretation of the Lord's Supper as the proclamation of the present and the coming Lord. Even if there were no historical connection between the passover and the Lord's Supper, it still remains a fact that the Synoptics directly, and John indirectly, want us to see this relation. They did not feel any hesitance about it.

The second possible objection, the reference to the words "This do in remembrance of me," must be examined with exactly the same understanding. The *anamnesis* is not a "remembrance" of something that lies in the past, as we might remember a friend or a relative who has died. The *anamnesis* command and the command to repeat the Lord's Supper are rather invitations to live actively as members of the community which knows that the time of salvation has begun with the Cross and Easter, and that they can partake in the meal with the Lord until He comes. The instruction to "repeat" and to "remember" refers to the whole communion service with all its parts (whatever they may be), and not only to the eating of the "elements." The participants do not "eat the elements," in order to be reminded of Christ, or in order to "remember" Him. On the contrary, they "remember Him," i.e., that He is presently among them, and therefore they do eat the elements, and speak and hear the appropriate words of petition, institution, thanksgiving, and praise.

The statements on these pages have been, of course, only a very short outline of a possible approach to a Biblical understanding of the Lord's Supper.[37] There was no intention of deny-

---

[36] Cf. also Theo Preiss, *op. cit.*, p. 85.

[37] The predominant element of proclamation is also present in Baptism. This is convincingly worked out in the article "Baptism and Evangelism," by Markus Barth, *Scottish Journal of Theology*, Vol. XII, No. 1, March 1959.

ing the relation between the wine and the blood of Christ, and
between the bread and His body. The passion, the Cross, and
the proclamation of the death of the Lord are of course present
in the New Testament texts on the Lord's Supper. However,
under no circumstances should these events be separated from
the Easter victory and the return of the Lord. The early community understood this inseparability and wanted us to understand it by way of its Biblical witness, which is our only source
of knowledge. What is accomplished in the death of the Lord
is made manifest in the victory of Easter, and in the hope and
joy of the expectation of the coming Lord. Precisely this accom-
plishment is proclaimed in the Lord's Supper of the New Testament community, and it must also dictate our conception of it.[38]

How does all this answer our basic question of the relation
between the Lord's Supper and the sermon? The two are not to
be set over against each other, for that would mean that the
same Jesus Christ gives Himself to the members of His body in
two different ways. Nor is it possible to say that the "action"
of the Lord's Supper is the visible Word of God, as distinct
from the invisible Word in the sermon. The usual term "Word
and sacrament," quoted so often in our Protestant churches, is
in fact without any Biblical support. It is the one life-giving
Word of God that is present in both the sermon and the Supper.
The dead word of the human sermon is made alive by the Holy
Spirit, calls the congregation to the forgiveness and life in Jesus
Christ, and promises His glorious return at the end of the days.
The dead and very human meal with bread and wine is made
alive by the Holy Spirit and allows the believers to celebrate in
communion with Christ the foretaste of the promised end and
goal of all their work and life. In one short formula, one can
perhaps say that the sermon offers life and promises eternal

[38] For an elaboration of this aspect see Theo Preiss, who calls "the
eschatological character" of the Lord's Supper basic in the New Testament,
op. cit., p. 91; see also pp. 93 ff.

union with Christ,[39] and that the Lord's Supper is the hour when this is already anticipated in faith and hope. Both are actions of proclamation of Jesus Christ. Only after having said this can one perhaps proceed to define carefully these two forms of the one Word of proclamation. The notion of a "symbol" has not been found to be helpful. The conception of a "sign" might lead to an understanding, but it has to be remembered that all these ideas stem from our own cultural and philosophical preconceptions and do not find much support from the Biblical texts.

Since the sermon and the Lord's Supper cannot be separated as two different activities of the Church, one must conclude that the Lord's Supper should be celebrated every Sunday. However, a worship without the Lord's Supper is not less "valuable" or valid, as if only a part of Christ were present in the sermon. To avoid this misunderstanding, it is justifiable to celebrate the Lord's Supper only once a month, as Calvin suggested.[40] This is not a principle, but a practical suggestion. The idea that the Lord's Supper should only be celebrated a few times a year, in order to give it a "more important place," is entirely nonsensical. On this basis, it would also be necessary to preach only a few times a year, in order not to "devaluate" the importance of the sermon.

The fact that the self-proclamation of Jesus Christ is made manifest in both the sermon and the Lord's Supper necessitates the conclusion that the Lord's Supper cannot be confined to the "officially gathered" congregation, while house services with sermons are permissible. House services for small groups of church

---

[39] 1 Corinthians 11 seems to indicate that the Corinthians had first a meal, then the Lord's Supper, and after that the sermon. Paul criticizes the Corinthians for not delaying the meal until all the brothers and sisters are present. He objects to beginning with the meal and only delaying the "sacrament." One can only have the sacrament if one is willing to share the meal with all the brethren. Other evidences in the New Testament are that the sermon came first and then the Lord's Supper, which order became the accepted order in the Church.

[40] Cf. Institutes, Book IV, Chapter XVII, Paragraph 43: "very frequently, and at least once in every week," but later Calvin (*Corpus Reformatorum*, 10 a 213) suggested monthly celebration.

members living in one neighborhood will become increasingly important in the future. Exegetically it is not possible to say that the Lord's Supper cannot be celebrated in those communities. With the exception of the evangelistic meeting or open teaching sermon, the Lord's Supper can be celebrated wherever a sermon can be preached. The conception that the Lord's Supper requires a consecrated church building, a church constitution, or the assembly of all the members of the congregation must be regarded as superstition. Nevertheless, after having agreed that there are no exegetical and dogmatical reasons for making rules with regard to these practices, one must establish a certain order in the church to avoid having each church member celebrate his own Lord's Supper. But these regulations cannot banish the Lord's Supper from the house service.

5. THE OFFICE OF PROCLAMATION

The separation between "clergy" and "laity" is but another form of separating the sermon from the "liturgy." Jesus Christ holds the office of proclamation, and it is the whole Church that participates in it. The risen Lord uses the whole Church for the service to His own work. The mission of the Church is the mission of Christ. The Church does not have a mission, but the Church is a mission, and it is performed by all members with their gifts of grace, which are given for the edification of the Church and the service to the unbelievers.

It might be argued that in a way it is easy to define the sermon and the Lord's Supper as the activity of the exalted Lord through the Holy Spirit. However, this question is still left unanswered: How and through whom is the presence of the living Lord made manifest? Furthermore, the statement that the presence of the Head of the Body, not just the "remembrance" of Jesus, constitutes worship, is, as one might say, easy to make, because it is correct and represents beyond any doubt the witness of the New Testament community. It was somehow more difficult to reach the conclusion that because of the hypostatic union with Christ we cannot ultimately separate the Word of God to man from the word of man to God. Jesus Christ in the Holy Spirit is the One who preaches Himself, and who enables man to accept what is being preached. Call and response, command and obedience, are both united in Jesus Christ. He Himself is at the same time the Preacher and the content of the sermon; He is also the obedient Man who stands in our place, who takes us into His prayer and intercedes for us as the heavenly High Priest. He makes Himself known, and in the sermon He invites His people to eat with Him at the Meal until the last day when He will eat and drink anew with His disciples in perfect union.

Jesus Christ holds the office of proclamation, but here the question arises: How does this concretely affect the structure of the Church? What does the union between Christ and His Church mean for the offices? In their witness the believers point to the One Word who is Jesus Christ, and by doing so they do not witness the One who is dead; they are witnesses to the resurrection of Jesus Christ. (Acts 1:22; 2:32; 3:15; 4:2; 4:10; 4:33.) They speak "in His name," which means that He Himself is present. They do not "refer" to Him or "remind" others of Him, but it is He Himself who speaks through them. But who are "they"?

The divine unity between call and response, sermon and prayer, the Lord and the Servant, must determine the worship service in spite of all human dualism, but this unity has been badly attacked in the history of the Church in order to give an answer to our question. There are many attempts to justify theologically a partition of the believers into "office bearers" and common people. This separation is signified by the terms "clergy" and "laity." It is but another form of separating the sermon from the "liturgy." Since the preacher is a man who belongs to the congregation, and also a man who has to speak *to* the congregation, the conclusion has been drawn that this double aspect constitutes a definite partition. The "liturgist's" favorite thought of splitting the worship service into the sermon and the "liturgy" has secretly entered into the Reformed Churches in the form of a split between the minister and the congregation. Many Reformed theologians reject the Lutheran and Episcopalian conception of the officers, even though they make the same mistake that they want to avoid, i.e., they simply extend the conception of the office to some more people, by including the elders and deacons in the group of especially qualified men. In this way they divide the Church into two parts. This partition cannot be excused by referring to the fact that the perfect union of the acting of Jesus Christ and our actions in the Church is only an eschatological promise, so that the "offices" which split the Church are temporarily necessary but not ultimately important.

Another basis must be found for the understanding of the "offices" in the Church. A pragmatical point of departure is impossible, for it would have to borrow its essential parts from the ancient mystery religions and from religions in general. The figure of the priest would stand at the center — the priest who is nearer to God than the masses of people, and who knows how to convey the divine truths to the ignorant. The desire to have such a priest is very old and very human. The priest confirms in the name of the godhead what I am thinking and doing; he warns me before I begin to think and to act; and he comforts me after I have failed to think and act rightly. But this cannot be the Biblical answer. This figure of the priest would usurp the power and the office of Christ Himself. The desire to have a Church that is organized and guided by that kind of priests indicates that the believers try to escape the living Christ and prefer a human substitute. This kind of thinking cannot lead to an understanding of the offices in the Church.

The proper point of departure is the office which is held by Jesus Christ. There is, strictly speaking, only one office in the Church; the office of Jesus Christ the High Priest. He is the only mediator, the only "office-bearer," who combines in one person the offices of the King, Prophet, and Priest, or whatever other office we might like to name. The Gospels, the Pauline corpus, and especially the Epistle to the Hebrews, indicate clearly that all of these Old Testament offices are perfected in Christ. (Hebrews 7:22-23, *et al.*) All the so-called offices in the Church must be understood as services to the one office, which is held by Jesus Christ. The whole Church which is formed by the Holy Spirit into one body with Christ, is the servant to this one office. There is no difference and discrimination between the members of this body.

"The prototype for the ministry is our Lord Himself," as J. K. S. Reid puts it.[41] Inasmuch as the action of God toward man and the obedience of man to God has been fulfilled in Christ, we are bound to say that Christ gives to His body what He is and what He has. The Church does not "receive" Christ's office or ministry, but it rather participates in it. It would be misleading to think in terms of quantities, as if the Church would take over "part" of His ministry or would reflect or represent partially what Christ is and does. The Church is not the *vicarius Christi.* Instead the Church participates in the whole ministry of Christ, so that Christ Himself is at work in the ministry of the whole Church. The most we can say is expressed in these statements of Alan Richardson: "because Christ is the Apostle, the Church is apostolic; because he is the High Priest, the Church is sacerdotal; because he is Servant, the Church is ministerial." But this can only be said because of the qualification that follows: "Christ himself is our Apostle, Priest and Deacon, and the missionary, priestly and ministerial functions of the Church are the ways in which he works through his body in the world."[42] It is He who works, and the work is in and for the world![43]

[41] *The Biblical Doctrine of the Ministry,* (Edinburgh: Oliver and Boyd, 1955) (Scottish Journal of Theology Occasional Papers No. 4), p. 1; it is, however, to be asked whether the second part of this sentence is fortunate: "the pattern for all the New Testament has to say about the ministry is what our Lord has to say about His ministry." Is really "what He says" the important point rather than what He "is" and "does"?

[42] *An Introduction to the Theology of the New Testament,* p. 291.

[43] Cf. also the second chapter of T. F. Torrance's *Royal Priesthood,* especially pp. 35-42.

It is the risen and exalted Lord Himself who in the Holy Spirit is present in the Church; who does not create the Word through the sermon, but the sermon through the Word; and who does not promise to come to a Church which is gathered together because of teaching and preaching, but rather makes the Church teach and preach because He is already with it, for He has called it together. The eternal Word existed before the Church did, and His ministry existed before the Church was called to participate in it. This participation cannot possibly be the special privilege of the "ministers"; it is the corporate ministry of the whole Church. It cannot be that only some men are invited to hear the life-giving Word in order to preach it to the masses of the ignorant believers; and this means in concrete terms that it cannot be that only the preachers learn and know how to read the Bible carefully in order to have priestly authority when it comes to teaching and preaching.

On the other hand, this participation of the Church in the ministry of Christ cannot mean that every church member is a "minister" or a pastor.[44] Everyone has a ministry, but not everyone is a minister. There is a striking similarity between the hierarchical Church, which distinguishes between priests and laymen, and the sect which claims that everyone is a pastor. Both conceptions indicate that the *charismata*, the grace gifts, are not taken seriously, or that they are only understood as a decoration of what the Church already is, in virtue of its constitution or self-understanding. "Are all apostles? Are all prophets? Are all teachers? Do all work miracles?" (1 Corinthians 12:29.) This would betray a quantitative conception of the Church's participation in the ministry of Christ, as if, so to speak, everyone had inherited "a piece" of all the offices which are united in the person of Jesus Christ. On the contrary, "His gifts were that some should be apostles, some prophets, some evangelists, some pastors and teachers, for the equipment of the saints, for the work of ministry, for building up the body of Christ." (Ephe-

[44] I have tried to elaborate this further in *Christ Our Life* (Edinburgh: Oliver and Boyd, 1960), pp. 40-70.

sians 4:11-12.) "All the members do not have the same function" (Romans 12:4), but each has been given his own *charisma*
for the edification of the Church. Real *individuality*, in that each
member has its special place and special function, can only be
realized in the Body of Christ. The mutual edification of the
members of the body abolishes *individualism* and uniformity.
All serve toward one end, by performing their different functions, "until we all attain to the unity of the faith and of the
knowledge of the Son of God, to mature manhood, to the measure of the stature of the fullness of Christ." (Ephesians 4:13.)
They all serve the one living Word and all their works, "inspired
by one and the same Spirit" (1 Corinthians 12:11), are participation in the office of proclamation. This corporate ministry
makes it impossible to think of the Church either as a group of
believers, in which only some people proclaim the Word of God,
or as a sect, in which everyone has the same function.

The "priesthood of all believers" has often been misunderstood in one of these ways. It has been said that everyone is
his own priest and has direct access to God the Father, via the
Mediator. This abstraction ignores the fact that a "priest" is quite
meaningless without his counterpart. What is a priest without his
partner? Or in more familiar language: What is a Christian without his brother? There cannot be a Christian without a brother.
There can be no edification, or up-building, without the corporate ministry, where one brother with his *charisma* is the
other brother's priest. Nor must we think only of this priesthood
of all believers in terms of an internal relation between believers.
The ministry of Jesus Christ is *for the world*, as is the ministry
of the royal priesthood of the "kingdom of priests" (Exodus
19:6), of which every member is a priest to "ten men from the
nations of every tongue" (Zechariah 8:23). This is how the
sacrifices of the members of the "spiritual house" in 1 Peter 2
must be understood. They had been Gentiles, but now they are
God's people, the *laos theou*, who have to "declare the wonderful
deeds of him who called" them. (1 Peter 2:9.) God establishes
this covenant, ultimately not because of these covenant people
but because of the people of the world: "I have given you as a

covenant to the people, a light to the nations, to open the eyes
that are blind." (Isaiah 42:6-7.)[45] The priesthood of all believers is, therefore, the corporate ministry of brother to brother,
as well as the ministry of proclamation and service to the unbelievers. For this reason the "unbelievers" and "outsiders" are
mentioned in 1 Corinthians 14, which speaks so intensively of
the charismatic functions within the Church.

This is, of course, not the place to discuss in detail the Biblical
doctrine of the offices. However, after these short quotations and
reflections it can be said in conclusion that the whole Church participates in the office of proclamation which Jesus Christ holds.
It does not mean that everyone is a pastor or a preacher, but it
does mean that all the *charismata* of the members of the body
serve to the end that "you may declare the wonderful deeds of
him who called you out of darkness into his marvelous light."
(1 Peter 2:9.) No church member is free of the responsibility
of proclamation, and no minister is free to claim that he alone
bears this responsibility. The Church cannot delegate the work
of proclamation to some of its members, for the Church can
only recognize that its whole work is a mission to the world,
and that this mission is performed by all members with their
charismata. As an illustration, it may be possible to draw a parallel in analogy to the understanding of the work of the triune
God. That is, the participation of the whole Church in the whole
office of Jesus Christ is made manifest by the work of the Holy
Spirit in the Church, in such a way that each member of the
Church has his *proprium* with his specific *charisma,* but so that
the one work of the one Church is not split into many little
works, which are separated from one another. One can even
speak of a *perichoresis*[46] of the various *charismata,* in order to
make it quite clear that these grace gifts are not functioning
in isolation.

To "bear one another's burdens" (Galatians 6:2) or to suffer
together if one member suffers (1 Corinthians 12:26) is but an-

[45] Cf. Markus Barth, "Der Zeugendienst der Gemeinde in der Welt," *Theologische Existenz heute,* No. 21 (Munich: Chr. Kaiser Verlag).
[46] Cf. p. 30.

other way of expressing the corporate ministry of the Church. A congregation is actually disobedient if it allows its minister to suffer unduly under the burden of his office of preaching. On the other hand, it is also disobedient if the members of the Church suffer from being forced always to be silent and passive as hearers of one and the same preacher, Sunday after Sunday.

While it is true that the work of the preacher cannot be replaced by other *charismata* of the church members, it is amazing to see what the New Testament texts[47] have to say about the active participation of many, if not all, of the worshipers in the New Testament community. "When you come together, each one has a hymn, a lesson, a revelation, a tongue, or an interpretation. Let all things be done for edification." (1 Corinthians 14:26.) Even if we do not dare to copy this form of worship in our worship services, and perhaps we ought not to try, this passage and similar textual evidences seriously challenge our practice of having normally only one man "perform" the worship service.[48] Without falling into sectarian type of worship, it should not be too difficult to let many members of the church participate actively in the worship service. Especially the young people and the new members can thus be taught very early that it is not the minister only who has a ministry.

These suggestions, however, do not help at the most important point. If the whole Church participates in the ministry of Christ, and if it is therefore the whole Church that has the office of proclamation, then it must very definitely be said that the preacher cannot be left alone with his sermon preparation. He can only preach after having heard the Word, but he cannot hear the Word when he is alone and isolated from his people in his study.[49] Hearing and preaching the Word is a process without

[47] Cf. also pp. 87-88.

[48] I have tried for many years in my own congregations to let the members alternately read the Scripture lesson or other parts of the service; we also had on Saturday night a "week closing service," which was conducted entirely by members of the church.

[49] Cf. the opening remarks in: David H. C. Read, *The Communication of the Gospel,* Warrack Lectures for 1951 (London: SCM Press, 1952).

an end, and it is a vicious circle that can only obediently be overcome in brotherhood.

The risen Lord Himself is ultimately responsible for the work of proclamation in the world through the Church. He uses the whole Church for the service to this work. The mission of the Church is the mission of Christ. The Church does not *have* a mission, but the Church *is* a mission. The whole Church is involved in this work.[50] Only after having said this can it now be said that there are relative differentiations between the members of the Church as "office-bearers." The work and the authority of these office-bearers are ultimately connected with the work of the apostles.[51] Since there is only one eternal Word which became flesh, the proclamation of the apostles cannot be qualitatively different from the proclamation of the preachers of our time. The difference consists, as Karl Barth puts it, only with regard to "space and time." It is one Word that is being preached, not because of the dedication, conversion, or conviction of the preachers, but rather because of the self-proclamation of Jesus Christ through the Holy Spirit. The difficult question of the apostolicity of the ministry of the Church cannot be discussed here. For our purpose it is only important to see that the position of the office-bearers cannot be defined in static and fixed terms, as if the difference between an office-bearer and another church member were of a qualitative nature. It would betray a static and dead conception of the Church to look at its structure, as if it were to be compared with a fixed photograph rather than an organic, growing, moving body which lives in time and moves in time like a motion picture film.[52] The Church is in motion and is moving toward a definite goal. Hence each new member of the Church can soon become an office-bearer or a bishop (like

[50] Cf. Bishop Lesslie Newbigin's very helpful little book *One Body, One Gospel, One World,* (London and New York: International Missionary Council, 1958), especially pp. 17 ff. and pp. 25 ff.
[51] Cf. J. K. S. Reid, *The Biblical Doctrine of the Ministry,* pp. 30-47.
[52] Here arises a difficult problem as to whether or not an elder should be ordained for life. It is not done in many European Reformed Churches, but the question is still left unanswered because the ministers are ordained for life, which constitutes an undue differentiation between elders and ministers.

Ambrose!).[53] Not too soon, however, "or he may be puffed up with conceit and fall into the condemnation of the devil." (1 Timothy 3:6.) The charismatic and even the institutional responsibilities cannot really be created by theological faculties or in evening courses for elders and deacons. The Church is not the product of education, like an army where only those who have served for a long time can occupy the higher and highest positions. The gifts and abilities are already present in the eternal election of the merciful God, who cares for His Church in His wisdom. The Church's task is obedient submission to His voice and careful recognition of the work of the Holy Spirit, in order not to hinder His work. Only after having accepted this situation can it be possible, and might it be necessary, to elaborate an understanding of the offices in the Church and of the necessary education for them.

Whatever one's specific conception of the characteristics of the ministry might be, it is possible and necessary for all non-Roman denominations to take the Reformer's Biblical interpretation seriously, that it is Jesus Christ who holds the office of proclamation, and that it is the whole Church that participates in it. The hearing and understanding of the Biblical Word cannot be an individualistic effort of the preacher. He cannot substitute his books or his ecclesiastical colleagues for his own congregation.[54] The members of his congregation with their *charismata* must share the preacher's work of preparing the sermon. The office of proclamation does not belong to the preacher but to the Church, because it is Jesus Christ's office. The sermon is not a special type of proclamation, distinct from the proclamation through works and various gifts of the church members; the sermon is the source and the heart of all the charismatic works which are performed by the members of the body, so that after this weekly activity a new sermon can be preached on Sunday.

[53] He was consecrated bishop and baptized at about the same time!
[54] It is highly problematical to arrange by church law that the ministers are not members of their local congregations, as if the presbyteries were a "higher," better, or more independent kind of Church, an *ecclesiola in ecclesia,* a little church within the church at large.

III The Sermon

1. THE CLAIM OF THE SERMON AND THE ACTIVITY OF THE HEARERS

The sermon is not a full and proper sermon because the words which come out of the preacher's mouth are true and Biblical. The sermon is an event in and of the Church. There is an inseparable relation between the proclamation and the congregation. But the preaching has priority over the hearing, inasmuch as the call has priority over the response. The sermon does not "come" from the experience of the minister or the daily life of the people; it "leads" to the daily life and the experience of it. The proclamation cannot be based on an analysis of the situation of the world, but it leads to an understanding of it.

The argument, as it was developed in the first two chapters, could be misinterpreted in a one-sided manner as leading to the abstract idea that preaching is a true sermon because of the words used. This conception is destroyed by the fact that the office of Jesus Christ is offered for participation not to the preacher alone but to the whole Church. Although the sermon depends utterly upon its faithfulness to the Bible, it cannot be said that the sermon as such is already a full and proper sermon just because the words which come out of the mouth of the preacher are true and Biblical. Francis of Assisi, who is said to have preached to the birds, actually did not preach a sermon; at best he spoke aloud his meditations. The sermon is an event in and of the Church; it is not a certain way of repeating Biblical messages irrespective of the presence of listeners.

This is the reason that the famous article VII of the *Confessio Augustana* connects the sermon and the sacraments with the

Church, which is defined as *"una sancta ecclesia perpetua mansura,"* one holy Church which remains in perpetuity. It is the *"congregatio sanctorum, in qua evangelium docetur, et recte administrantur sacramenta,"* the assembly of saints in which the Gospel is truly preached and the sacraments are truly administered. The main point is the inseparable relation between the proclamation and the congregation. No sermon without a congregation, and no congregation without a sermon!

After having appreciated this statement, it is tempting to criticize it. The phrases *"recte docetur"* and *"recte administrantur"* lend themselves, one might say, to the conception that a true *("recte")* sermon not only constitutes the Church, but *is* the Church, as if the correctness of the sermon and of the administration of the sacraments were the criterion for the life of the Church. The *Confessio Augustana* does not intend to say this in its context, but as soon as a misunderstanding of this kind arises one is forced to make the contrary statement as a corrective: the Church is where the sermon is truly *heard* and where the sacraments are truly *received.*

Speaking and hearing belong together, just as proclamation and prayer, call and response, command and obedience, and the deity and the humanity of Jesus Christ belong together. Nevertheless, there remains a priority of preaching *(recte docetur)* over hearing, inasmuch as the call has priority over the response. The two belong together, but not in such a way that a true sermon can be preached only if people really listen. There can be a call without a response and there can be a sermon without a result of faith and life, but with a result of opposition, neutrality, and judgment. Because of the obedient response which has been made by the man Jesus, the lack of response in the Church today can never mean that the Church's work has reached its end. A congregation that does not respond still stands on the basis of the once and for all response and obedience of Jesus Christ. Were this not so, all preaching and working in the Church would be impossible and would automatically turn into religiosity, which appeals to a hidden kernel of goodness within man, in order to make it active and useful for worship.

To understand the power and claim of the sermon, one must necessarily begin with the Word, the call, and the proclamation, because of the priority of the sermon over the faithful response of the people, and because the obedience of Christ overshadows the disobedience of the people who do not respond faithfully. First, we must be concerned with the content of the sermon, and only secondly can we deal with the situation of the Church and its people. But it remains true that the sermon is not a naked, abstract, and impersonal address, which works *ex opere operato;* it is an event that takes place in the Church because the preacher is a man of the Church who lives with his people during the week, and also because the whole Church participates in the office of proclamation. The work of the preacher does not depend only upon the Holy Spirit as He is present in the minister's study during the days before the sermon is delivered, but primarily upon the Holy Spirit as He is present during the hour of worship, when He works as the translator between the preacher and the congregation. If metaphors are to be used, it would be wiser to say that the Holy Spirit is located in the space between the pulpit and the pews than to say that He is located in the heart of the preacher.

If the sermon is an event in the Church, does this not lead to the dangerous error that the sermon is *only for* the Church? In answering, a distinction must be drawn[1] between a special evangelization and the normal Sunday sermon.[2] Although the Sunday sermon is to be prepared and delivered by the preacher with the consciousness that his hearers are Christians and not pagans, the sermon is a public and not a private event. "What I tell you in the dark, utter in the light; and what you hear whispered, proclaim upon the housetops." (Matthew 10:27; cf. John 18:20.) The sermon does not address the Church alone, but neither does it speak to the absent outsiders. It is this strongest

[1] Cf. Newbigin, *One Body, One Gospel, One World*, p. 22.
[2] Ultimately, this distinction is arbitrary, but it is a factual phenomenon in the Church, and it might be better sometimes to take it more seriously in order not to confuse the different tasks of evangelizing and building up a congregation; the references to the "milk" and the "strong meat" (1 Corinthians 3:2; Hebrews 5:12-14) belong in this context.

(almost illogical) thought, which points directly to the corporate ministry of the Church. Strictly speaking, the church members cannot say "our preacher's sermon," but they must be able to see why they can truly say "our sermon." The sermon is the proclamation of the Church; it is, of course, not the only way in which the Church proclaims, but it is the normative proclamation. All other proclaiming acts and words flow out of the sermon. It is, therefore, abstract and false to say that the sermon "works" only during the hour of worship, or that it is only concerned with the people present. It addresses those who are present, but it is concerned with those who are not present, i.e., those among whom the church members will be living during the coming week. The demand that the sermon should "come" from the fullness of the experience of the everyday life is quite naive and one-sided. It should not *come* from there, but it should *lead* to it. The sermon must come from the living Word of God, as it is made known to us in the witness of the Bible. Other sources for the content of the sermon are merely illustrations, and it can be asked whether the Bible itself does not offer enough of these illustrative materials. Since the Bible is not a collection of eternal and timeless truths but rather a book of the history of God with His people, the point could very well be made that the whole Bible is an illustration which, in all its parts and varieties of reports, is more than sufficient for illustrations. This concreteness of the Bible forbids *eo ipso* an abstract sermon.

As distinct from evangelization, the sermon is an event which takes place in the Church. More simply, the sermon is an event *in and of* the Church, while evangelization is an act *of* the Church. But it is outside of the knowledge and control of the Church and its workers to say when evangelization creates a congregation, and when it does not. The preacher and the people of the Church cannot decide who hears the sermon and accepts the message. The Church cannot find out where its own limits are, i.e., where the "non-church" begins. The Lord of the Church will reveal it at the last day.

It is undoubtedly true, as is often said, that the Church must find quite new ways for its life and work.[3] We can no longer uncritically maintain the old thought patterns and conventional forms of church activity. Nevertheless, a mistake can be made by overemphasizing this, thus escaping into a world of dreams about a better and a more modern Church in the future. Before we are ready to talk about new forms of preaching we should rather learn to use the "old" forms properly. The most urgent concern is surely not for more modern language, more pleasant buildings, and better communication, but rather for a more burning interest in the Word of God by the ministers and their co-workers in our churches. There is no special gospel for the "modern man," as if we had to discover the means of communication first, before we dared to preach it. The Word of God is still the Word of the God of Abraham, Isaac, and Jacob, and it is a new Word each day when it is preached and heard. This Word is not dependent on the history and situation of the world. Inasmuch as the preaching of the Word of God cannot possibly be separated from the thought, world, problems, and situations of its hearers (and must therefore be highly political), the very content of the sermon does not *come from* the world with all its questions and problems, but from the living God *into* this world.

The Bible texts, which are our sermon texts, are intimately connected with historical events. God spoke and acted in history with His people. The proclamation of His Word will again create new situations in the history of God's people; the promise is that the Word will, literally speaking, "make history." The first ground rule in homiletics is to trust in this promise. Preaching is to depend utterly on the power of the Word which is being preached. This trust in the power of the Word is not merely an intellectual or spiritual readiness to believe that the Word is "true," but

[3] I have experimented (because of 1 Corinthians 14:26) with allowing the congregation to interrupt the preacher, not so much with critical questions of knowledge, but with statements of support and further additions to the concrete application of the text. This is only possible if there are good co-workers in the Church, and even then it is dangerous. There are other ways of breaking away from the old patterns.

in a very radical way the assurance that something will really "happen," and that the Word will accomplish what it has promised.

The lack of trust in the absolute priority and dependability of the Word is the main reason for the increasing interest of the Churches and their "experts" in the techniques of speech, communication, illustration, and rhetoric. A true preacher will feel ashamed to be called a "great preacher." He will learn to view in a new light even the smallest beginnings of life and faith in his Church. Knowing that all preaching is only possible on the basis of the success that is already accomplished, although hidden, even from the eyes of the believer, he will not wait to see success, and he will not calculate on it. The Church is free from the necessity of thinking in terms of purpose and success, plan and goal. The Church is also free from bondage to a certain language or terminology, but it can receive its language and terms of expression daily from the Word that is proclaimed. The proclaimed Word not only addresses, calls, sustains, and saves those who are the "objects" of the mission and preaching of the Church, but it also keeps the Church itself alive to perform this mission. It is, therefore, not quite correct to call the Church an "instrument" of the work of Jesus Christ in His world. The Church's existence is not merely instrumental, as is for instance, a hammer which is used to drive nails into wood; rather those who proclaim are also addressed by the very Word they proclaim. The Word works like a "hammer," not only through but primarily *for* and in the witnessing Church.

It is clear that the preacher is not permitted to preach what his people like to hear. While he can let them sing hymns which they like, even this should be done with great care. The Word which breaks through the sermon cannot conform to the ideas of the people who preach and who hear it. Only the lack of trust in the authority of the Word, or the brutal intention to preach an "extraordinary" sermon deliberately to shock the congregation, can drive people away from Christ. The authentic sermon will draw those people to Christ whom He has called, and it will push those away whose hearts He has hardened, "to one a fragrance from death to death, to the other a fragrance from life to life." (2 Corinthians 2:16.) It is not the business of the preacher to try to force this result or even to speculate about it. The preacher gives himself entirely into the hands of the Lord, whose Word he proclaims. The sermon demands both hearing and speaking. Indeed, the Word itself demands these human activities, for speaking and hearing are not caused by the desires or the needs of the people. We do not preach because people want to hear us, nor do we proclaim the Word because we have analyzed the world and have come to the conclusion that the world needs to hear the proclamation.

Speaking and hearing belong together, so that there can be no preacher who has not heard the Word and no hearer who can remain silent. Since it is not possible to be a hearer in privacy without the brotherhood of believers, it must be the intention of all preachers to belong to a circle of members of the Church, with whom he hears the Word before he preaches it. There is no direct route from the privacy of the study to the pulpit. Sharing the daily life of the congregation is a poor substitute for the corporate studying and hearing of the Word. The sharing of experiences, the mutual exchange of thoughts, and the works of love are surely indispensable, but they can never take the place of the corporate preparation of the sermon in the studying of the sermon text. The office of proclamation belongs to the whole Church and not just to the preacher!

All the following remarks on the preparation of the sermon must be seen from the viewpoint of this corporate ministry of the Church. The hearing, which is the readiness to be judged by the Word, and the speaking, which is the willingness to speak out with joy what one has heard, are the calling of the whole Church. The Church will have to be ready to hear and to speak against its own will and plan, as well as against the desire and expectation of those who might come to the Church for the first time in their lives, and whom one might not like to lose or discourage. It is the risen Christ Himself who encourages, invites, and preserves those who hear His Word. Through Him the Holy Spirit makes the application of His Word, and only secondarily does the minister learn in obedient listening to the Word how his sermon can be a real "application," and not merely an exegetical lecture. In order not to be abstract when speaking about the sermon, one must always keep in mind that the sermon — for all its uniqueness — is an event that is repeated more than fifty times a year. It is not because of practical reasons, but rather because of the living and moving function of the real life in the Church, that a single sermon cannot contain all doctrinal wisdom, or the totality of the Biblical witness, or, what is worse, the "essence" of the Bible. Obediently heard and preached, each passage *is* the totality of the voice of the living Christ. His voice cannot be split into parts, so it must not be the concern of the preacher to draw a complete picture of God's plan and history with His people. The Church is in motion; the hearers of the Word are on the road; and they are moving toward the day of fulfillment. What they do not hear and learn today will be given to them tomorrow. They do not perform their mission in a nervous haste; they will have patience to wait until the return of the Lord. Their waiting from one Sunday sermon to the next reflects their hope for the last day. "You have need of endurance, so that you may do the will of God and receive what is promised. 'For yet a little while, and the coming one shall come and shall not tarry.'" (Hebrews 10:36-37.)

2. THE BASIC UNDERSTANDING OF EXPOSITORY PREACHING

The "art of preaching" is only free of rules, principles, and methodological recipes when it is based on the prophetic and apostolic witness. The sermon is determined by the text, and it cannot be summarized, as if it were possible to point to the "essence" of what God wants to speak through the sermon text. This conception of verse-by-verse preaching, as it was re-discovered a generation ago, is still basic for all homiletical work. New avenues for a theological understanding of Biblical preaching cannot lead away from this "classical" approach; they can only make it more radical.

There are no rules, prescriptions, and principles for preparing and delivering a sermon. This statement does not merely express a "feeling"; the reason that it is not possible to elaborate and teach principles and methods for the preparation and delivery of the sermon can be stated quite clearly.[4] Since preaching is the action of the Father in the Son through the Holy Spirit in the Church by means of human voices, this action cannot be controlled and regulated by systems and thoughts of these human tools. The "method" of one preacher cannot be adopted by another preacher; and each preacher must ask himself whether he has become the victim of his own method, and whether it is not high time that he re-examine his approach and change it radically. The ways in which God wants to work cannot be systematized.

It is clear that "what we preach is not ourselves, but Jesus Christ as Lord" (2 Corinthians 4:5), and that it cannot be done "in lofty words or wisdom" and "not in plausible words of wisdom, but in demonstration of the Spirit and power, that your faith might not rest in the wisdom of men but in the power of God" (1 Corinthians 2:1, 4-5). Christ is more important than all our experiences and theological thoughts; He is also more important than the Biblical texts, for we do not preach the Bible, we preach Christ. But where else other than in the Biblical witness do we hear what God has done and has promised to do? " 'What no eye has seen, nor ear heard, nor the

[4] Cf. the book *On the Preparation and Delivery of Sermons* by John A. Broadus and Jesse Burton Weatherspoon (New York: Harper & Brothers, 1870, 1943), which is an attempt to provide these prescriptions. One cannot help feeling that the authors were perfectly aware of the impossibility of their undertaking and that for this reason they offer a great variety of suggestions, so the reader is depressed by the multitude of warnings, hints, and rules without which preaching should not be attempted. A great number of modern books are in line with this "classical" textbook of the last generation.

heart of man conceived, what God has prepared for those who love him,' God has revealed to us through the Spirit" (1 Corinthians 2:9-10), which is the witness of the books of the Bible. It is this second form of the Word of God that demands to be preached through the power of the Spirit, because it is God's free will to give this promise and to act according to it.

Preaching is "free," i.e., without rules, principles, and methodological recipes only if it is done on Scriptural grounds. And the contrary is true also; if preaching be separated from a Scripture text ("free" in this disobedient sense), it is not free but demands rules and psychological and rhetorical laws, etc.[5] It never has been and it never will be possible to preach an authentic sermon that does not grow out of a passage of the Bible. The Word of God in this first form is not another word alongside of the Word of God in the second form. The "art of preaching" is only free when it is based on the prophetic and apostolic witness. There are now a great number of valuable books which have pointed out clearly why only a Biblical sermon can be considered to be an authoritative and authentic sermon, through which the congregation receives the food that it needs for its life and work.[6]

[5] A look into the history of preaching demonstrates this point very clearly. The influence of Roman rhetoric caused a mode of preaching known as "topical preaching"; the more widespread topical preaching became, the greater was the emphasis on principles and rules. Augustine's *De Doctrina Christiana* and later Bonaventura's *Ars Concionandi*, with its formalism, are landmarks in this development. The short special study by Harry Caplan, "Classical Rhetoric and the Medieval Theory of Preaching," *Classical Philology*, April 1933, No. 2, pp. 73 ff., gives depressing examples of what has been done in preaching. Many new books in the field of homiletics are not too far removed from the medieval perversions of preaching.

[6] Some of these publications which date back to the 1930's have greatly helped the European and Asiatic Churches during the times of war and crisis. Some examples of more recent representatives of this understanding of the sermon are, for instance: A. Schädelin, *Die Rechte Predigt* (Zürich: Zwingli Verlag, 1953); Wolfgang Trillhaas, *Evangelische Predigtlehre* (Munich: Chr. Kaiser Verlag, 1935, 1955); A. C. Craig, *Preaching in a Scientific Age* (London: SCM Press, 1954); Julius Schieder, *Unsere Predigt* (Munich: Kaiser Verlag, 1957); and, somewhat different in style and approach, James T. Cleland, *The True and Lively Word* (New York: Charles Scribner's Sons, 1954); also the books by Donald G. Miller and D. T. Niles.

This new understanding, which is widely accepted in Europe and has been deepened during the German Church struggle and the crises in other countries in Europe, is in many ways based on the new interpretation of the function of theology in the Church as it was begun by Karl Barth and Eduard Thurneysen a generation ago. It has introduced a certain "conception of the sermon," which is now almost fixed and static and therefore not quite without dangers. This has become particularly obvious since the discussion about the theological work of Rudolf Bultmann has spread over almost the whole *ecumene*. It is as though the understanding of the sermon which prevailed in the 1930's had been driven to a defensive position, which can undoubtedly lead to an unfortunate fixation or scholasticism in the conception of Biblical preaching. The crisis has not really come yet, but it is already approaching in many Churches. There is no reason for lamentation, anxiety, or even heresy trials (although this is not quite unheard of in Europe), but there is some urgency to rethink the position of those who advocated expository preaching from pre-war times. Their understanding of preaching, which is still the basis of homiletics, can be outlined as follows.

a. Topical preaching or the preaching on "religious subjects" is, with good reason, despised and is characterized as merely human talk, or a kind of theological lecture that has no more authority than that which lies within the preacher. And this, according to the Scriptures, cannot be considered a sermon.

b. The sermon is clearly based on a passage of Scripture, which is read immediately before the sermon, so that hymns, announcements, and the collection of money do not separate the sermon text from the actual sermon. The sermon text itself is not so short that the sermon becomes more important than the text, nor is the text so long that the sermon could only deal with very few aspects of the text.[7]

[7] It is interesting to see, for instance, that Dietrich Bonhoeffer used to preach in the early 1930's on very short texts, as many of his contemporaries did. This method was discarded later, when it became usual to preach

c. The sermon is totally determined by the text. The thoughts of the text govern the thoughts of the sermon. Ordinarily the sermon begins with the beginning of the text and ends with the concluding verse. The preacher cannot go "behind" the text to discover and summarize the "essence" of it, but he must take it in its canonical form, as it is written in the Bible.

d. The old idea of trying to find a *scopus* of the text, the "essence" as it were, is rejected as a dogmatical presupposition which is brought to the text from the outside. The sermon should say what the text says. The length of the sermon should also be determined by the text.

e. The sermon has no title which would appear in the newspaper or the church bulletin. The attempt to find a title for a sermon means that one feels able to summarize what God wants to speak through the sermon text. Only if the sermon text is already known under an obvious title, e.g., "The Prodigal Son," can a title be used, but these titles do not indicate the "content" or climax of the message; they merely locate the Bible passage.

f. The sermon, however, is not an exegesis which goes from verse to verse. This exegesis is only a necessary step in the preparation of the sermon. The sermon goes beyond that. It is not a mere homily, which puts equal weight on each verse, but it brings out the inner movement, tension, and climax of the passage. This is not the *scopus* of the text, but rather its "message." During the preparation, the exegesis leads to the question: What does God want to say through this text? It is this message that has to come out in the sermon. Few passages begin with this climax, most of them lead to it, and this is also what has to happen in the sermon. Historical remarks, cross references, archeological proofs, and specific explanations[8] of

on longer texts. The discovery that not only the content but also the form and sequence of the verses of the text is important is expressed in the short introduction to Barth and Thurneysen's collection of sermons, *Die Grosse Barmherzigkeit.* It should be clear, of course, that sermons on the Ten Commandments, on the petitions of the Lord's Prayer, etc., are perfectly possible. In these cases, the sermon text would be short.

[8] E.g., the remark that the disciples were not sitting at the table but

points of the sermon text are to be used only if they really con-
tribute something necessary for the understanding of what the
text wants to say to the congregation. In order to reach an understanding of the "message" of the text, each verse has to be taken
seriously, realizing that the Biblical writers knew what they
were doing when they did not leave out the context but reported
many concrete details. No Bible text allows a crystallization of
a timeless truth out of the context and the sequence of the
verses, although parts of the wisdom literature are perhaps
an exception.

g. The "application" is not banished to "part three" of the
sermon, for ideally each sentence of the sermon is explication
and application at the same time. The question (toward the
end of the sermon): "What does this mean for us?" and the
whole approach which makes this question necessary are totally
rejected. It betrays the fact that the first part of the sermon was
quite irrelevant and unnecessary. True preaching, verse by verse,
leading to the message of the good news of the text, implies this
question: What does this mean for us? Remarks on the witness
of the Bible, without leading directly to this question, are considered to be mere repetitions of the Biblical witness. They might
be useful in Bible study hours or teaching meetings, but not
during the hour of corporate worship of the congregation. The
congregation need not artificially and rhetorically be persuaded
that the preached word is valid and relevant to the modern man.
The whole sermon as such *is* the "modern" witness on the basis
of the Biblical witness.

h. It is not necessary to use the words of the text or to quote
verses. On the contrary, the tendency is not to waste time establishing connections between the Biblical Word and our modern
language but to go right ahead in our own modern way of

---

lying; that there was much salt at the banks of the Dead Sea (Matthew
5:13); that washing a guest's feet was done in most houses; that the road
to Jericho was, and still is, dangerous; that the "eye of a needle" (Matthew
19:24 and parallels) is a small gate in the city wall; and other architectural
and linguistic explanations.

expression. Thus we avoid the intellectual complications which arise when the gap of the famous "two thousand years" between the Bible and the "modern man" dominates the sermon. However, this does not mean that "churchly" language should be avoided, or that the words of the text or other parts of the Bible should not be mentioned or quoted. There are certain words for which others cannot be substituted, which is a true reflection of the fact that the Good News as such does not fit into the thought patterns of the old Adam.

i. Illustrations are seldom used, and then with great care lest the hearers remember the illustrations and not what they were intended to illustrate. Comparisons or short examples are always preferred to illustrations and stories. Apologetic tendencies are avoided, and least of all is the sermon considered to be a means of defending the Church. Instead the sermon judges and criticizes the Church and its activity. Likewise, statements and elaborations on "what one should not believe," on errors, heresies, and misconceptions are absent from a true sermon. The sermon is "positive"; it is not a debate on standpoints or convictions.

This understanding of what a Biblical sermon should be is certainly very realistic and solid. It has been taught (as far as this is possible) and practiced in many churches; it has led to a real revival of the life of congregations; and it has opened the way for a new understanding of the actuality and authority of the Word of God, as it is witnessed to in the books of the Bible. It has proved that a sermon is not "interesting" because it offers many clever illustrations, emphatic appeals, and emotional exhortations, but that the most interesting and "sensational" sermon that can be preached is one according to this understanding of preaching. It goes without saying that the preacher, in order to be able to preach such a sermon, must be a solid exegete and must not be afraid of hard work for the preparation of his sermon. He must have a sincere respect for the Biblical Word and a deep trust that the Word will accomplish what it promises. He must learn the discipline of a ministry with daily contact with the Bible and with a high regard for the theological work of exegesis, for which he was trained. He must also know the thoughts, interests, and forms of expression of his congregation, so that he is constantly driven back to the Biblical Word and from there again back to his congregation.

Many benefits would accrue if this understanding of preaching were accepted and practiced by the preachers of our time. There is no better way than this to drive the young preachers away from the unchristian adoration of pulpit heroes, and from the unintelligent interest in homiletical books which offer a variety of recipes for effective preaching, or even from "sermon outlines" with accompanying illustrations. A preacher who disciplines himself to preach Biblical sermons will feel ashamed to spend his time with these things, for it will be a matter of his own personal honor and integrity not to be tempted to strive for ideals to which he was not called and commissioned. Least of all will he use other preacher's sermons or even parts of sermons, for "I am against the prophets, says the LORD, who steal my words from one another." (Jeremiah 23:30.) Biblical preaching, as it was outlined on the previous pages, should certainly be practiced by all young preachers for at least the first five to eight years of their ministry. Only after many years of faithful preaching with this kind of approach can the preacher see the hidden weaknesses of it. If he has kept up with his daily exegesis and theological study of the fathers and the modern authors, he might be able to go a step further. He will not give up any parts of this way of preaching, but he will make some of the thoughts more specific and push them further.

In order to see why it is necessary to go beyond the understanding of preaching of the 1930's, it may be useful to point out some of the impasses which will result from it. If one really preaches verse by verse leading up to the climax of the message of the text, then it follows inevitably that the sermon will be one-sided. It will not be possible to use other parts of the Bible in order to fill in the gaps and to balance the message. The question of the choice of the sermon text is, therefore, extremely important and not merely a subcategory of homiletics. It be-

comes almost the main question. At this point, the advocates
of this kind of expository sermon escape, as it were, and add
two suggestions to their conception of preaching, as it was summarized above. Realizing this one-sidedness, they argue that
each sermon should present, at least to some extent, the Good
News of the Cross, of Easter, and of the Second Advent, as the
central events to which all the texts of the Old and New Testaments directly or indirectly bear witness. The preaching of these
central events is, so they say, the only reason that we preach
at all, and it is conceivable that some people may sit in the
church for the first time in their lives or for the last time. No
one should come to church without hearing the proclamation
of these main events, and anyone who has been to church
can die during the coming week and should not therefore leave
the church without having been reassured of the reality of
these events. This is the first argument. The second is that the
preacher, if he is an honest exegete, must realize that this
"Christology" is not literally expressed in every sermon text,
and that it is often not possible to add or to develop the Good
News of the Cross, Easter, and the Second Advent without
doing violence to the sermon text. The suggestion is, therefore,
to balance with "liturgy" what the sermon has not been able
to express. Hymns, Scripture readings, and prayers have to fill
in what is lacking in the sermon.

These two suggestions have to be taken very seriously and
must not be wrongly identified with the naive attempt to "pack"
the whole of systematic theology into one worship service.
Nevertheless, the question must be raised whether or not this
understanding betrays the conception of the worship service
as something like a "divine drama" that has to be complete in
itself. Is not the presupposition here that the preaching of the
witness of one passage requires some additional sources, which
are considered to be necessary to make it perfect? And is not
this conception identical with the idea that the Cross and the
other Christological events are only preached if they are literally
mentioned and verbally spoken out? The question arises here

whether "a text" can be *pars pro toto* of the message of the Bible, or whether one needs some foreknowledge or criterion from the outside to make the text "speak." This question becomes particularly acute in preaching on Old Testament passages.

The following considerations are an attempt to go beyond this basic understanding of expository preaching. The difficulties which arise out of it have to be kept in mind, but the basic importance and value of it should not be minimized. The new avenue for a theological understanding of Biblical preaching cannot lead away from the approach of the 1930's; it can only make it more radical, and this will lead to some very practical conclusions.

3. THE CREATION OF HISTORY
   THROUGH THE SERMON

The sermon is an instrument for the creation of history. The Word which we are called to preach is in itself the promise that the hidden majesty of the Bible is revealed at the hour of the sermon. The triune God wants to make Himself known on the basis of the words which have prophesied and witnessed to His Son. The sermon text has the "self-will" to allow this embodiment of God in the assembled congregation. The sermon does not merely describe the movement from the text to the people, but is in itself this movement.

To find an answer to the question whether a specific passage of the Bible can be *pars pro toto* for the whole message, the basic question must be faced first: what should happen while a sermon is being preached? If preaching is not the only way of proclaiming the Good News (cf. Matthew 5:16; 1 Peter 2:12 *et al.*), although it is the normative way, it should be possible to point out what is actually happening during and through the sermon that cannot happen elsewhere. The point of departure for the whole complex of questions was the doctrine of the three forms of the Word of God and the "Trinitarian analogy." The specific question has to be dealt with now in the light of what has been said in the first two chapters. Attention is again focused on the "second form" of the Word of God, the written witness; for it is only through this Biblical witness that the Church can hear and preach a sermon and can test the word of the sermon by going back to this written witness. (It goes without saying, of course, that those who operate on the basis of "natural theology" cannot in the least agree with any aspect of the arguments used here; their position is rather similar to what might be called "spiritualism," which enables a man to make any statement without being forced to explain or prove it. It is then possible to preach on any "subject" and simply to claim divine authority for it.) It is no other than Jesus Christ Himself who is witnessed to by the written Word of the Bible, and it is the same witness with which we are concerned when we try to understand how the risen Christ wants to make Himself known through the preaching of one particular passage. What then should happen by (and during) the sermon? On the basis of the previous considerations, the answer must be: God's history with His people. The term is of course not of importance, and any other one could be substituted for it. It is only used here because it has become a *terminus technicus* in present theology. It expresses the fact that God has not ceased to be a God of action; that the Bible is not the end of a "sacred history"; that Jesus Christ is not dead but the risen Christ who works with His Church in the world. His self-proclamation is not an intellectual or spiritual conception, but an acting that makes itself manifest in very concrete events.[9]

If the sermon is understood as a text sermon, one is driven to the conclusion that a certain Bible text, which in itself is the reflection of "God's history with His people," must again create such history, or else it is a dead text (but who would dare to say that?); otherwise the sermon has not been a real Biblical

[9] I have tried to unfold this more clearly in an article "The Theological Significance of History," *Austin Seminary Bulletin*, Austin, Texas, April 1960.

sermon. The sermon should be the instrument for the creation of history. How can this be done? Or in other words: do we need a hermeneutical principle which enables us to exegete the text in a special way so that such history will happen?

It seems possible to look to the history of Israel in order to find an answer.[10] Israel's proclamation centered around the feasts as a "descriptive representation (*darstellende Vergegenwärtigung*, Martin Noth) of what God had done in the past. This pattern could perhaps be used for the understanding of how the unique and unrepeatable actions of God in the past could be celebrated now in our Sunday services, so that God could again create such history. One could also suggest a look at the very Early Church, in order to see what the early Christians thought about proclamation. Here one would not have to fear the complications which arise with regard to the history and the self-understanding of Israel, because the Early Church did not have as long a history to look back upon as did Israel. However, both approaches would be quite misleading. We cannot copy the *Vergegenwärtigung* that was performed and believed in Israel, nor can we go back to the self-understanding of the Early Church and simply adopt it. The self-understanding of Israel or the Early Church cannot constitute the self-understanding of the Church and its proclamation. The continuity between them and us, between the Old Testament and the New Testament, is not guaranteed in the self-understanding of the believers. To define one's understanding of the sermon on that basis would lead inevitably to the notion of a "sacred drama," which has already been rejected. The question has obviously been wrongly asked.

It is true that each passage of the Old and the New Testaments is directly or indirectly the result of concrete preaching, teaching, or proclaiming. But it would be quite wrong, also, to

[10] Cf. p. 113; Martin Noth, "Die Vergegenwärtigung des Alten Testaments in der Verkündigung," *Evangelische Theologie*, July/August 1952, pp. 6 ff.; also Gerhard von Rad, *Theologie des Alten Testaments* (Munich: Chr. Kaiser Verlag, 1957), Vol. I., pp. 127 ff., 135 ff.; and Claus Westermann, *Zur Auslegung des Alten Testaments*, in "Vergegenwärtigung."

approach the Bible with the intention of crystallizing out of a given text the probable "sermon" which might have been the origin of it. If we followed this procedure, we would deny the uniqueness of God's history, for we would make it relative even though we had the intention of "making" it absolute. The "wonderful deeds" of God, to declare which the people of God are called (1 Peter 2:9), would be made timeless by this process of dehistorizing, but the human witness in all its worldliness would be made absolute. The Bible would then take the place of God, and God would be reduced to an idea which lies behind the Bible. This is just the opposite of what was intended.[11]

The point of departure for homiletical work with the text cannot be anthropological or historical; it must be strictly theological. It is the triune God Himself who wants to make Himself known, and who wants to make His promise again true that His Word is a living Word; that is to say, who wants to reveal Himself. With regard to the Old Testament, where the problem becomes most acute, Gerhard von Rad expresses the point of departure (Ansatz) in this way: ". . . the faith that it is one and the same God who has revealed Himself in Christ and has also imprinted His footsteps in the history of the Old Testament covenant people, so that we are faced with one proclamation of God, here to the fathers through the prophets, and there to us through Christ, (Hebrews 1:1)."[12] When we ask for the guarantor of the continuity between the Old Testament and the New Testament, between the Early Church and our Church, we cannot point to the people, their situations, and their understanding of themselves; we must see that it is one and the same God who asks His people again and again to hear His Word and to participate in the revealing work of Christ. The con-

[11] The effort to find out what the original setting of a given text may have been is, however, by no means absurd. This approach of the form critics is extremely helpful, not only for the interpretation of a passage but also in connection with the problem of the choice of sermon texts, cf. pp. 163 ff.

[12] Von Rad, "Typologische Auslegung des Alten Testaments," Evangelische Theologie, July/August 1952, p. 31, my translation.

tinuity is in Him. This thought coincides with the conclusions reached at the end of the first chapter. We can now say that one must speak of a "homiletical principle" rather than a hermeneutical one, when it comes to the actual preparation of the sermon. The Word which we are called to preach is in itself the promise that the hidden majesty of the Bible is revealed at the hour of the worship service and sermon. The triune God wants to make Himself known on the basis of these words which have prophesied and witnessed to His Son. More simply, the sermon text "has the self-will" to cause this embodiment of God in the assembled congregation.

It has to be admitted that this conception of the work accomplished by the sermon can be called a "preconception" and can as such be criticized. But it is precisely the same thought which is expressed in the order 1-2-3 of the forms of the Word of God.[13] The "preconception" (for all its dangers!) means that one takes seriously the fact that the preparation of the sermon is not performed outside of the Church or in a "neutral" field of merely scientific exegesis, but indeed inside of the Church as the work of the Church under the promise of the Holy Spirit. The preacher who prepares his sermon must see that he has taken his stand right within the Church, which confesses that this "presupposition" is not an intellectual construction but the very creed of the Church. To put it in different language: the preacher is not called upon to find out each Friday, when studying his sermon text, that the statement that Jesus Christ is not dead but risen is not a lie but the truth. He must not approach his sermon text with an artificial scientific skepticism. If he is well prepared through the life and work with the fellow Christians in his congregation, he can approach his sermon text in all confidence, with the understanding that the promise is true that Christ wants to reveal Himself through the sermon on this text. This does not mean, of course, that the preacher knows in advance what he must preach, or that he could rely on some

[13] See pp. 29 ff.

theological truth which allows him to approach his text without the readiness to be totally challenged and surprised by his own sermon text. But it is much better to prepare a sermon with the confidence that this "homiletical presupposition" is really a true expression of the promise of God than to try to preach a sermon that "brings in" Christ's Cross, Resurrection and Second Advent in a way that does injustice to the text. The simple fact *that* a sermon is preached, and *that* it concentrates on one specific passage, indicates that the sermon comes from the great events of Christ; there can be no law to the effect that these events have to be mentioned in each sermon.

The task of sermon preparation will be to find out where and how and in what form the text "wants" to break through to the proclamation. It must be from the text through the word of witness that God Himself appears in grace and judgment, consolation and edification, admonition and warning. Therefore, it can be said that the sermon is the movement from *this* text to *these* people. It is not appropriate to say, as it is often expressed, that the preacher stands between the text and the people. The preacher is no mediator. He is not the one who has to "get something across." He must observe the inner tension and movement (the "self-will") within the text which is directed toward the hearers. The news which God brings forth out of the text is Good News, so that the preacher can, soon after he has completed his careful linguistic preparation, search for this Good News. What happens in the sermon, then, is good and merciful, because the congregation will be taken by it into the way of Christ. If one cannot hear that the sermon is "good" — better, stronger, and more joyful than anything the world can offer — the sermon has not been a truly Biblical sermon.

Our human attempts to "portray" God's grace will always be one-sided, even if we try to perfect and polish them into balanced systematic thoughts. Once it is agreed that preaching cannot be a "summary of the Bible," each sermon text can be confidently viewed as *pars pro toto* for the Biblical witness.

4. THE RESPONSIBILITY FOR
SELECTING THE SERMON TEXT

Since the whole Church participates in the office which Jesus Christ holds, it cannot be the preacher alone who selects the sermon text and who prepares his sermon in privacy. The Church is responsible for the decision to choose a lectionary or the texts for a series of sermons, and the preacher must share the burden and joy of the sermon preparation with members of his congregation. But toward the end of the week the preacher is alone with the Word. He must be ready to preach against the expectation of the congregation and against his own will.

If it is true that a limited passage of the Bible, a sermon text, is of such importance, the burning question becomes: How and by whom should the text be selected? There are three suggestions:

The advocates of the "Christian Year" and of an enforced lectionary (e.g., in some parts of the Lutheran and Episcopal churches) say that they have already solved the problem and given the answer. It is certainly good for the preacher simply to be confronted with a given passage. Then he will not pick out his favorite Bible texts to escape difficulties, e.g., to avoid texts on predestination, the Ascension, the baptism of Jesus, the transfiguration, certain passages in Hebrews, or whole books in the Old Testament. The pericope of the lectionary disciplines him to face texts which might be far remote from his own "devotional life" and intellectual preference. He will stand, so to speak, under the text and not above the text. However, just because the lectionary is healthy for the preacher does not necessarily mean that it is good for the congregation. It can make the congregation passive. Moreover, the lectionary as a program according to the "Christian Year" is, strictly speaking, nothing else than a "sacred drama" extended over the period of a whole year. This becomes quite clear in the arguments which Gustaf Wingren[14] uses to defend the lectionary. In addition to this, it has to be asked who should bear the responsibility for the proclamation on the basis of this particular text, if one can simply consult a list in order to see what one has to preach? Who has authority to say that all congregations within a Church or a country or even all over the world, in East and West, in the city and in the country, must hear a sermon from the same text? Serious people will hardly assume that the unity of the Church could be guaranteed by the technique of having the same sermon text, prescribed hymns, and Scripture readings. Indeed, must not one church hear today the end of Romans 8, while another must urgently be invited to hear Matthew 24, or a word of judgment from Jeremiah? How can this choice be decided by the tradition of the lectionary?[15] Moreover, the lectionary implies the danger of picking out "important" parts of the Bible, whereby the Old Testament usually falls short. Who could judge what the "important" passages of the Bible are? If one wanted to maintain the strict Biblical sermon, which deals with one and not with many texts at the same time, the lectionary cannot be considered a solution of the problem; the question is just pushed one step further.

There is a second suggestion which is known as *lectio continua*, the series of sermons on parts or whole books of the Bible over the period of many Sundays. Known in the early Greek Church, this custom was adopted by the Reformers, especially Calvin and Bullinger. The advantage is that one book of the Bible is closely studied and preached, and the life of the Church can concentrate around the message of this book. Instead of preaching through all the chapters of one book, it is, of course, also possible to preach a series on specific passages across the Bible, e.g., the accounts of the calling of the prophets and the disciples, or the service of the women in the church, or the

[14] Wingren, *Die Predigt*, p. 248 f.

[15] It has been necessary in many of the younger Churches which grew out of mission Churches, to write yearly lectionaries for the purpose of simplifying the work of exegetical aids or conferences for the inexperienced preachers. This is, of course, quite a different case.

priestly function of Israel and of the Church toward the Gentiles, etc. Then the congregation knows in advance the sermon text and is not intellectually surprised by it; the proclamation on Sunday does not jump from one part of the Bible to another, which is normally the case when the preacher follows a lectionary (only the Christian Year provides some continuity, but even this requires switching from Isaiah to Paul and back to Genesis). The obvious disadvantage of the *lectio continua* is that after a few Sundays the congregation may live in a different situation and may have to face quite new problems, yet it has to follow the "program." The preacher will then be tempted to add here and there "relevant" remarks to his sermon in order to meet the demand of the present hour. Political tensions, new developments in racial relations in the community, or internal difficulties and changes within the congregation may make it difficult to preach faithfully the passage which "comes next" in the *lectio continua*. The preacher will be liable to the criticism that he arbitrarily "mixes" politics with his proclamation; and this criticism is not unsubstantiated if it were obvious that his sermon text did not really speak to the current issue or concrete problem. Were our world more peaceful and its developments in the social and political life more regular and stable, the *lectio continua* would certainly be healthy for the preacher and the congregation, and it would indeed be the answer to the problem of selecting the sermon text. This regularity and stability exists only within a close community, which lives and works toward a definite goal that can be defined in clear terms — for instance the work of a theological seminary during the time of a semester can and must follow a fixed "program." This objection, however, should not lead to the opposite extreme, as if the preacher had to pick out passages which match literally the political situation, e.g., that he preaches on passages concerning Egypt at the time of trouble in the Near East (which really happened in some congregations during the Suez crisis!). One cannot lose trust in the wonderful promise that the sermon will create history even in a turbulent world, and that the sermon cannot depend

on the history of the world. The conclusion will probably be
that the minister and his co-workers will have to decide again
and again on a short *lectio continua* (approximately for the time
of one month),[16] which is to be preferred to the irregularity of
the lectionary, that changes from one part of Scriptures to another and bypasses many passages. It should be the task of the
church session to meet weekly to criticize last Sunday's sermon
and to help the preacher with the preliminary preparation of
the next sermon; and to decide monthly the texts for the *lectio
continua*. The monthly Communion service would establish an
organic rhythm in the change of the *lectio continua*. If the church
session is not willing to accept this task, the preacher can very
well co-operate with a Bible class or a youth group. The co-
workers in each congregation will have to decide between *lectio
continua* and new texts for each Sunday. It is obvious that a
series of sermons is very unsuitable in a holiday resort church,
where the congregation changes from Sunday to Sunday. And
preaching according to a lectionary is very unwise if there is a
certain guarantee that the same congregation will be present for
many Sundays, in which case *lectio continua* is preferable. One
cannot find a dogmatical or Biblical criterion that leads to a
definite solution of the problem. The important thing, theologically and ecclesiologically, is that the selection of the text
be understood not as the business of the preacher alone, but
primarily as the responsibility of the workers in the congregation. The congregation must participate in the minister's
responsibility.

There is a third suggestion which is unfortunately accepted
by most preachers. It is known as the "free choice of the text."
The minister alone chooses his sermon text according to his
own understanding of the "needs" of his congregation. This
method is by far the most dangerous one. It would be justified
only if the minister could consult his congregation each week,

---

[16] I would no longer attempt to preach for 22 Sundays on John's Apocalypse, as I did some years ago, except in a series of evening services,
which are more in the line of teaching sermons.

which is practically impossible. The minister's feeling of the needs of his people is too subjective a basis for the proclamation. It means not only that the minister overestimates his own knowledge (for how could he really know what his people "need"?), but it is also basically a thought that begins at the wrong end. The need of man to hear the Word of God cannot be the motivation of the work and words of the herald, least of all when it comes to the specific question of the text one should take as the starting point for the proclamation on Sunday.[17] The "free choice of the text" is not substantially different from the topical sermon or from the sermon on a "subject," even if the preacher tries to preach a truly Biblical sermon. In a way he claims to know in advance what he wants to preach. He either has a "subject" in mind and tries to find a suitable text for it, or he has personally been impressed by a certain text and feels that his congregation should share this experience with him. In either case he usurps an authority which is not his. He claims to stand vicariously for the whole Church. Could one then be proud of being a minister in the Reformed Church, which has done away with pope and priests, if he were to do exactly the same by making a decision which is as authoritarian as the hierarchical priesthood is? And it is in a way more dangerous, for the Roman priest officiates according to the lectionary system which has been elaborated by the Church, and which looks back to a long tradition; he is less an individualist who usurps authority than is the Reformed preacher who decides by himself what his people need.

The whole Church participates in the office which Jesus Christ holds. The Church, which lives through the Word, serves the Word. The distinctions between offices and responsibilities are

[17] The situation is, of course, quite different in pastoral counseling, where the minister in his relation with one or two individuals must really try to understand the "needs" and the whole situation of the persons concerned; here it is really a necessity to know the Bible so well that he need not consult his church session, in order to know the chapter at which he must open his Bible to read and unfold the Word which the people really "need" to hear!

only of a relative nature.[18] Inasmuch as the sermon must be called "Word of God" in faithful acceptance of the promise, so it must also be called "word of the Church," and not just "word of the minister." The Lord of the Church not only demands obedient response, but all response is offered on the basis of His obedience which is offered on behalf of all. This is what the Church expressed by speaking about the "hypostatic union."[19] The congregation must not only say "our minister," as if he were a special representative of Christ and could never be reached by the "laity," but they must also be able to say "our sermon." The word of the Church as God's Word is not just the word of some consecrated or ordained men, but really the word of the Church.

The sermon text, therefore, grows out of the relationship between the minister and the congregation. The choice must come from contacts in Bible studies, house visits, and session meetings. The preacher has to live with his text through the whole week; that is, not in privacy, but in brotherhood with his people in the Church. No preacher should avoid sharing the sermon text with as many people as possible. Not only should this be done for the purpose of "training" people to listen correctly and with better understanding to a sermon (although this will automatically also be true), but primarily because of the fact that the Word which is preached on Sunday is, although an entirely new and authoritative word, already the Word by which the Church has lived during the week. To deny this is an undue separation between "the Word" and Jesus Christ. The preacher preaches to people in the Church. Were this not true, how could he pray with them and confess the faith? One must get away from the understanding of the sermon as an event that takes place only once. The Church lives from Sunday to Sunday, from sermon to sermon, and from one Lord's Supper to another Lord's Supper. We would deny and distrust last Sunday's sermon if we thought we had to begin each Sunday with

[18] Cf. pp. 117-126.
[19] Cf. pp. 67 ff., 107-108.

a pagan congregation. There are very many references in the Epistles, Gospels, and in the Old Testament clearly pointing to "the gospel which you received." (Cf. Galatians 1:9 as only one example.)

The preacher's knowledge of the Bible and of his specific tools for exegesis cannot be his priestly and secret wisdom. He should inform as many co-workers and church members as possible about these necessary parts of his daily work. Experience shows that there is more interest in the churches in such information as time is made available and patience is demonstrated by the pastor for such instruction. If those tools and theological books are hidden and not explained to interested people in the Church, the lexica, commentaries, and concordances, and the historical and dogmatical books will soon be despised as academic hobbies of the preacher, or they will be the object of adoration for those who believe that books contain more wisdom than the Bible. The minister himself will fall into these errors which are inspired by the congregation. Practice proves that many preachers have already become the victims of the first of the two approaches, namely that they themselves despise their theological tools.

When the preacher shares his own study of the sermon texts with his people it will be quite natural that his own weaknesses will be seen, and that he cannot any longer be the celebrated preacher and theologian in this superficial sense of the word. But he will be a good theologian when he shares his questions and answers with his people and when he receives new questions and answers from them. This situation is the beginning of real brotherhood under the Word. Since it is impossible for any human being or institution to find a valid and "once and for all" perfect exegesis of the Bible, it will again and again happen that the preacher has to confess his ignorance, even in the pulpit, about certain parts and verses of the Bible.

Those church members who live with their minister under the Word should select with him the passages for the Sunday sermon, as well as the topics and subjects for the teaching courses in the church. It can be done either by reaching an agreement about a *lectio continua* or by deciding on a lectionary for a certain period of time.[20] If willing co-workers have not yet been found it is also possible to use the textual material provided by the educational boards of the Churches for study in Sunday schools and to preach on those texts which have recently been studied. This is particularly helpful for guest preachers, unless they are called upon to preach clear teaching sermons or give evangelistic addresses, which, of course, cannot be compared with the regular work of the minister.

In sharing the preacher's burden, all people of the church are called to serve with their *charismata* for the edification of the church.[21] This will enable the preacher and the people to find the obedient answer to the question as to which text or series of texts should be chosen for the sermons, and it will strengthen the preacher invaluably.

But all this does not mean that it is in the last analysis the church which preaches the sermon to itself. Only one is called to be the preacher. The last part of the sermon preparation, and above all the delivery of the sermon, is the minister's own work. A sermon cannot be prepared in the last stage by many or even by two people. Toward the end of the week the preacher is quite alone with the Word. It may then be discovered that the sermon has to be preached in quite a different way than he and his people had thought. This is the freedom of the Word, or, as it is often expressed, "the prophetic ministry" of the preacher.[22] The minister must be ready to preach against the will of his people, and against his own will and desire, if the Word wants him to do this. But even then, the preacher knows that there are people in the church who lived with him under this text and who will be called into obedience by this text, even if it

[20] I have tried this for quite a long time and have seen that it is practically possible. Those who share with the preacher the responsibility of proclaiming the Word will also, quite naturally, be his critics, and this is of extreme importance.
[21] Cf. the excellent remarks on this subject in D. T. Niles' books.
[22] Cf. E. Gordon Rupp, *Prophetic Preaching*, Joseph Smith Memorial Lecture (Birmingham: The Berean Press, 1954).

runs counter to their understanding and anticipation. It is un-realistic, of course, to assume that there will ever be a congrega-tion in which very many members will see their responsibility of participation in the ministry of proclamation. Likewise, it will seldom happen that the session of the church, as the natural group of co-workers, will readily agree to study the sermon text with their minister. Very often the preacher feels that he is left alone with one or two members or with his wife only. But he will have to see that this is not as it should be, and that the first step toward an improvement is not the effort to learn better techniques of preaching, but rather the hard and patient work with the members of the church who are naturally in authority (the "office-bearers" or the members of the youth groups, who are expected to become responsible Christians in future years). It is ultimately the Word itself that makes this selection, which would lead the minister into many difficulties if he had to decide whom he should invite. There remain still many practical problems; but they cannot be answered by escaping to the one-man system, which, psychologically speak-ing, would indeed help to avoid a great many complications. A parallel problem, that space does not permit to be discussed in this book, arises with the question of how the minister should find people with whom he can pray. It would be equally false either never to pray with members of one's Church (or only to do so to "help" them) or to flee to other ministers. The harsh "law of practical theology" cannot be bypassed: the more obedient the practical performance of one's ministry is, the more dangerous it is in terms of human misunderstandings; whereas the less one dares to do, the higher will one's position be in public opinion.

5. THE ONE-SIDEDNESS OF THE SERMON

A Bible text "wants" to be preached in such a way that the same God who spoke and acted in Israel and in the Early Church, as it is recorded in this text, will speak and act again during the church service. It is the task of preaching to make this action known and to allow the "history of Christ with His Church" to happen, which is of significance for the life of the whole world. The preaching of a passage does not demand balancing or harmonizing one text with another. The canonical form of the sermon text in it's one-sidedness must determine the sermon and the whole service.

After all that has been said, it should now be possible to make a series of final statements on the understanding of a Biblical sermon, thus leading somehow beyond the conception of preaching of the 1930's and yet solidly based on it. Much criticism has been made of "topical preaching," and fun has been poked at "preaching on subjects." Nevertheless, the supporters of these methods that were flourishing especially in the nineteenth century have a certain concern that should not prematurely be overlooked. It is obvious that the desire for "topical sermons" arose mainly for two reasons. There is, first, a desperation on the part of the preacher when he realizes that it is impossible to preach "everything" in one sermon; the material must be limited, or else a twenty- or thirty-minute sermon can simply not be preached. There is, second, the psychological consideration that one single point would be accepted and remembered by the congregation much easier than many points or thoughts. These two arguments are not meaningless, and Biblical preaching must now be examined to find out whether it would not *eo ipso* meet these problems without being forced to fall into the error of topical preaching.

First, reference has to be made to the limited possibility of distinguishing preaching from teaching. Obviously a prophetic word of the Bible will create a sermon very different from a sermon preached on a passage of the Pastoral Epistles. One must seriously question whether it is at all possible to preach a true sermon on the textual basis of a typical "teaching" passage of the Bible, e.g., parts of the Epistles. Should one not save those passages for the teaching sermons, or special evening or week-

day services? There is no real reason why the presupposition of
the classical understanding of expository preaching should be
accepted, namely the strange idea that it is theoretically possible
to preach on any passage of the Bible. Is this not the origin of
many difficulties?

However, it can be said that those typical *didache* passages
or admonitions were written on the basis of sermons which were
actually preached in the New Testament community, and likewise in Israel. Historical and form criticism often make it possible to reconstruct a probable sermon "behind" the *didache*
passage. But it is not by accident that these passages have
come to us in the form of doctrinal or *didache* texts. One has to
perceive at this point the analogy between the canon and the
sermon conception as the given dimensions, and as the frame-
work, within which the Word presents itself in its second and
first forms. To go "behind" the canon, in order to find "better"
material for preaching, is analogous to the attempt to go "behind" the sermon and analyze it with the intent of distinguishing sharply between the preacher's "own thoughts" and God's
thoughts. The task of the preacher cannot be to examine his
text in order to find an *ipsissima vox* of Jesus, Peter, Paul, etc.,[23]
which would then be used as an "instant sermon." To draw
again the analogy to the sermon: one might have the desire to
summarize the sermon or to formulate the "essence" of the
sermon and give it a title. These procedures would indicate that
the preacher and the people are completely confused about the
three forms of the Word, and that they are not ready to take
seriously the written form, i.e., the canonical Bible in all its
humanity and with all its contradictions. Here is the weak
point of "demythologization" with regard to preaching, because
the attempt to crystallize something out of the context (as necessary as this might often be) can easily lead to the idea that the
Word is "undressed" of its time-bound, human form and is thus
no longer the Word of witness to the humiliated Jesus Christ
in His humanity. The texts in their canonical form are the

[23] Cf. pp. 32, 35, 110.

"material" for the sermons. This does not mean that the texts are simply to be read at face value. On the contrary, their canonical form can often only be fully understood after the exegetical and form critical work has been done. But after the completion of this work, the preacher must go back to the canonical forms in which the texts have come to us, be it as historical, prophetic, parenetic, or teaching text. Assuming (for the sake of simplicity) that there are the two main categories of kerygmatic and didactic texts,[24] each one should be understood and read as it presents itself. Why should teaching passages be "turned into" sermons, if it is agreed that a sermon is not identical with teaching, explaining, and expounding?

There are therefore good reasons for preferring "historical" or kerygmatic texts of the Bible for our ordinary Sunday sermons, for those texts that report "God's history with His people" will again create such history. By preaching these texts, the purpose is certainly not to persuade the hearers to believe that they themselves "are" Abraham, Jacob, Daniel, Mary, or Paul. Phrases such as "Are we not all like Paul?" or "Don't you see that we are all in this boat with Jesus and the fearful disciples?" indicate that the preacher does not understand that God's history is unrepeatable, and that it is not the "situation" or the faith of God's people which guarantee the continuity of God's love and plan with His people. We are not at all like Abraham or Paul; we are completely different. My relation to these men is not a possible similarity (which is not unthinkable) of our feelings in specific situations, but merely that fact that it is the same God who addresses, invites, and forgives us. This acting of God, reported in the passages which give an account of God's calling, judging, and forgiving, will happen again according to the promise. And this leads to the conclusion that these passages are the "ideal" sermon texts. The same God who acted with the fathers will act again in Jesus Christ through the Holy Spirit. If all our previous considerations are not false, a definition can now be attempted: "Historical" texts "want" to be preached in such a

[24] Cf. the more careful distinction on pp. 100-101, 103.

way that the same God who spoke and acted in Israel and in the Early Church, as it is recorded in these texts, will speak and act again during the church service, and it is the task of preaching to make this acting known and to allow it to happen. The "history of God with His people" is in the time of the Church very specifically the "history of Christ with His Church," which is of significance for the life of the whole world.

These "historical" texts can primarily be found in the historical books of the Old Testament, the prophets, the Synoptics, John, and Acts. Naturally this division is only true as a broad and rough generalization. There are many parenetic passages in the prophets and many "historical" parts in the Epistles. But it should be recognized that texts which directly record God's speaking and acting are "natural" sermon texts. Other texts ought to be preferred for teaching sermons or Scripture readings with a short explanatory introduction. Of course, this can never be a law. Each church in its own time will reach different conclusions regarding these characteristics of specific passages, but neither can one make it a law that a sermon *can* be preached on any passage of the Bible. Even if this were theoretically possible, why should extremely difficult texts be chosen when others offer themselves much more readily?

To take seriously the self-intent of each passage, as it is understood within its context, implies also that the canonical form of a certain text cannot be balanced with a parallel passage, which might be found elsewhere in the Bible. This procedure would be perfectly in order in teaching and Bible study, and it is of course a necessary part of the preacher's preparation. But the preacher will have to make up his mind very clearly whether he will preach Mark's or Luke's account or Matthew's report when he preaches on a synoptic passage, for the different accounts will create different sermons. Balancing one text with the other would lead, if it were properly done, to a theological lecture.

Inasmuch as there is only one Word of God, so there is only one true proclamation, which is based on the written prophetic and apostolic witness. Each passage of this written witness has its peculiar function in serving to proclaim the one Word of God, Christ Himself, whether it be teaching, preaching, or other categories, such as admonition, exhortation, prophecy, appeal, or instruction; each passage is a full and valid witness of God's will to reveal Himself at this specific time when this specific passage begins to speak. If this "self-will" of the passage is not seen, the preparation of the sermon is not completed, or the right sermon text has not been selected for this time and for this church.

In other words, the preacher will work on the text with the obedient readiness to find out where and in what way this text wants to become a sermon. It will then not be necessary to balance the message of the text with harmonizing statements in the sermon, or with hymns, prayers, and Scripture readings. On the contrary, all parts of the worship service, including the Lord's Supper, will serve this one message of the text.[25] Everything that happens on Sunday will sharpen the profile of this one message since it is not the purpose of the worship to produce a "sacred drama" of the whole history of salvation, or to present a well-balanced systematic theology.[26]

Some examples must be given. If the text is an account of Jesus' baptism and stresses a particular aspect of Christology, it will not be necessary to balance this one-sidedness with other aspects of Christology. Single passages and whole books of the New Testament provide clear examples that the Biblical witnesses themselves had no intention of systematizing their witness. If a text speaks of the humiliated Lord, His fear and agony in Gethsemane, it will suffice to refer briefly and strongly to the fact that this is the same Jesus Christ who is the exalted Lord, but it will not be the task to make the message of the sermon

---

[25] The hymns cannot possibly be selected by someone who does not know the sermon text, as is often done.

[26] This does not mean, of course, that parallel passages in the Old and New Testaments should not be mentioned during the sermon. On the contrary, they can often be of great importance in bringing out more clearly the message of the sermon text.

"relative" by balancing it with opposite statements; the evangelists also refrain from doing this. If a text says that the Lord comes to His people, this fact shall be preached. However, if the text invites people to come to the Lord, this invitation shall be the message of the sermon and of the whole service. To preach both messages at the same time is to preach no message, because it will either lead to the idea that God and man both approach one another and meet half-way, or it will mean that the preacher presents a complicated dialectic to the congregation. Both are equally false. The one-sidedness of the service must be so clear that the congregation will, so to speak, "tremble" and wait eagerly for the next Sunday service. This must not be a "problematic" tension, which confuses people and leads to illogical conclusions, but it should be a true reflection of the one-sidedness of the Scriptures. A "synopsis" of the Synoptics and John, of Ephesians and Colossians, of some psalms and the Proverbs, etc., may be possible and necessary in a seminary, or in Sunday school, but this is quite out of place in the pulpit. The living Word is one-sided, and yet it is the whole Word. It is concrete and alive, and not part of a system.[27]

It is worthwhile to study the texts with the awareness that each text was spoken (and written) to a specific situation. Such investigations are not only a matter of historical honesty; they can also lead to a more serious understanding of the context, in which a specific passage wants to be used in the present proclamation of the Church. The parables, for instance, were spoken to Jesus' opponents and originally not to the disciples, although some Synoptic accounts apply them to the Church. Would it not be meaningful to prefer parables (and passages with a similar intent) for evangelization, rather than to use the 23rd Psalm, which was surely not written to be read in mass meetings? Again, this can by no means be a law. Parables can,

[27] It is always tempting for the preacher to concentrate on possible visitors and therefore to try to systematize the living Word and to balance it with doctrinal statements in order to present a kind of "introduction to the Christian faith" each Sunday morning.

of course, be preached in any type of congregation and at most intimate conferences or retreats. However, one is inevitably driven to the daring statement that there are Bible passages which are clearly addressed to the "outside," i.e., to the public at large, and others which are directed to those who are already working in the Church. By using the texts contrary to their own intention, one does violence to the texts, or adds something from the outside to them. It is certainly not wise, and in a way not honest either, to take a passage out of its obvious context and to apply to it a completely different set of questions (this is one of the dangers of preaching on very short texts). By looking at the traditions in Israel and at the Synoptic Gospels, one can observe how each witness has used the tradition in a specific way. The task is not to copy these Biblical witnesses with a false kind of Biblicism, but to understand the history of traditions and the approach of form criticism which have certainly taught a lesson that is not only valid for Biblical scholarship but primarily for the working preacher.[28]

If all this is true, then the old ideal of expository preaching must be revised or at least qualified. The old method of verse-by-verse preaching with the intent of working out the climax of the passage, is surely very good. But the hidden idea behind it was that each passage can theoretically lead to only one correct sermon, which can then be preached in almost any Church. This theory does not really take into account the fact that the sermon does not only come to the Church but that it also comes from the Church. It is probably more realistic, as well as Christologically more correct, to say that each passage can lead to a number of different sermons. The ideal that the sermon must begin with the first and end with the last verse must be revised, although this approach must always be considered the best "school of preaching." But the fact cannot be

---

[28] This can be seen so clearly that one can sometimes reconstruct the concrete situation of the Church to which the evangelist was writing; e.g., Krister Stendahl, *The School of St. Matthew* (Uppsala: C. W. K. Gleerup, 1954), especially pp. 20-35.

debated away that each passage has its peculiar "opening," i.e., the verse or the word which indicates clearly that *here* the passage wants to break through to the proclamation. This verse or group of words must not necessarily be the same at all times and in all places, although one has to be careful not to say that the "content" of the sermon depends on the "situation" of the congregation. The Word cannot depend upon the situation, but the situation upon the Word. But since the Word is not caught in the text, as if it were the prisoner of the sermon text and not the living and exalted Lord, no rules can be given as to the way in which the text should confront the congregation. This is the clearest expression of the fact that the situation depends on the Word and not vice versa. It is the free act of God to speak to His people through the sermon.

This "opening" of the passage constitutes the one-sidedness of the sermon and of the whole service. Thus the omission of some parts of the sermon text becomes possible and almost inevitable. Briefly the logical difference between the old expository sermon and this "one-sided sermon" can perhaps be formulated like this: the classical approach uses each verse of the passage to lead to the climax, i.e., the message of the passage; the "one-sided" approach comes from the climax, i.e., the message of the passage (the "opening"), to throw light on all the other verses and to lead to the understanding of them. The exegetical preparation is the same in either case, but the second approach dares to go a step further, because of the participation of the members of the church in the selection and study of the sermon text. Therefore, this one-sided approach can hardly be applied if the preacher is still left alone with the burden of preparing the sermon. If he has not yet found people to share with him the study, prayer, and meditation on the texts which they have selected together, he would go too far in using the one-sided sermon and worship service.

The one-sided service meets the requirements of the advocates of the topical sermon, even though it comes from an opposite starting point. Christ proclaims Himself through the sermon in one way, not in many ways and forms at the same time. This proclamation will create a healthy tension and longing.

6. THE PROBLEM OF CHRISTOLOGY AND OF PREACHING OLD TESTAMENT TEXTS

Not all texts of the New Testament, and strictly speaking none in the Old, express a direct Christology. There are three general approaches to the problem of the preaching of these texts: a typology that is concerned with specific "types"; a typology that receives the whole Bible from the hands of Christ; and a way of interpretation that avoids typology but refers to the human response in the Biblical texts, thus presupposing a Trinitarian point of departure and an ecclesiological conception of the reasons for reading the Old Testament in the Christian Church. The three ways are not mutually exclusive. The specific sermon text must determine the method.

It has been said that the Old Testament bears witness (consciously or unconsciously) to the expectation of the Messiah, and that the New Testament witnesses to the incarnation, ministry, death, and resurrection of Jesus Christ, so that all proclamation in the Church is embraced by these two great events: the coming of the Lord and His coming again.[29] The sermon is the human witness of sinful men, through whom God Himself speaks into this time of mortal life, which is determined by the Incarnation and the Second Advent, and which is signified by baptism and the Lord's Supper.[30] The preacher must see this "horizon" of the covenant, otherwise he will not serve the Word as he ought. All who hear the sermon (and the preacher himself) come from the reconciling act of God and are going for-

[29] Cf. the fine collection of sermons by T. F. Torrance with this title: *Christ Comes and Comes Again* (London: Hodder and Stoughton, 1958).

[30] This analogy is drawn by Karl Barth in his short and beautiful article on preaching, "Die Gemeindemässigkeit der Predigt," published from a transcribed address in *Evangelische Theologie*, 1956, Vol. XVI, pp. 194 ff.

ward to the redemption. The preacher must not only think but also proclaim this. But how can it be done if the particular sermon text does not explicitly say it?

This problem arises with both Old and New Testament texts, but it is more acute for Old Testament texts. The complications can be seen there more clearly, although it is evident that many parts of the New Testament also do not directly refer to the saving acts of God in Christ. It would not be very helpful to treat these New Testament passages "Christologically" simply because they "belong" to the New and not to the Old Testament. This treatment would indicate that one refers to the self-understanding of the New Testament community and uses it as a starting point for Christology. Even if this procedure were sometimes legitimate, historical and critical investigations could in many cases provide proof that this "Christian self-consciousness" is often not sufficient as a basis for a "Christological sermon." Generally speaking, this will be true for the whole of the Old Testament, unless one would like to refer to the passages which are clearly molded by a distinct consciousness of messianic expectation. There would then be the danger that the preacher might feel compelled to select only these passages. The danger of this approach should be illustrated clearly enough by the liberal theology of the previous generation, where it was widely accepted that Isaiah 53 and similar passages were practically the only Old Testament texts which could be used directly in the Christian Church. This should serve as a warning not to examine the Old Testament only from the viewpoint of its conscious and outspoken messianic theology in order to rule out all the rest of it as merely "Jewish" or "oriental religion."

The most promising attempt to avoid this mistake, as well as to escape a naive Biblicism which refuses (because of a lack of honesty) even to see the problem, is the approach which is known as "typology," and which is widely discussed among scholars and preachers. The typological approach is as old as the Biblical texts, for the Bible itself uses it. It has been used since the time of the Early Church fathers, although almost always bordering on the dangerous method of "allegory," with which it has often been identified.[31] After the last war, typology became one of the central questions in Old Testament scholarship. Gerhard von Rad's commentary on Genesis (1949), and the famous discussion on hermeneutics,[32] looking toward a common hermeneutical basis for the preparation of a new series of commentaries, are turning points in a new development of the understanding of typology and Old Testament hermeneutics in general, after these questions had been posed by Wilhelm Vischer in the 1930's. Practically all Old Testament scholars are now directly or indirectly involved in the discussion.

This is not the place to add one more voice to the many competent articles and books which have dealt with this subject in the international discussion. While the debate has by no means led to a conclusion or to an agreement on the heremeneutical question, the negative connotation, with which "typology" used to be mentioned and discredited, has almost disappeared. It has been widely recognized that the typological method is not to be considered as wishful thinking alien to the texts, but that it helps to understand the texts and to prevent a kind of interpretation that is only concerned with the singularity of the text, while it loses sight of the totality of the Bible and of the context of a particular passage or tradition. Typological analogies between the Old and the New Testaments are legitimate because of the election and call of the Covenant people, whose witness and response to God's actions have been made manifest in historical documents, which cannot properly be understood apart from these actions of God. This does not allow an identification (in the sense of one to one correspondence) of the "types" which we find in the texts, or of the old and the new Covenants. In that way God's actings would be "de-historized" and turned into

[31] A summary of the whole question is given in *Essays on Typology* by G. W. H. Lampe and K. J. Woollcombe, Studies in Biblical Theology (Naperville, Ill.: Alec R. Allenson, 1957).

[32] Cf. the double issue of the *Evangelische Theologie* July/August 1952, and the booklet "Vergegenwärtigung" which have already been mentioned.

a timeless system, into which one could enter quite arbitrarily at any point of the Bible. By doing this, one would deny the whole meaning of prophecy, expectancy, and fulfillment; in one word, one would deny history. Properly used, typology safeguards against such misunderstandings. H. W. Wolff has applied these results of Old Testament research to homiletics in a highly interesting outline in a short introduction to a collection of sermons. The outline is available in English translation[33] and is of basic value for the discussion of the problem. But before all these essays were published, Dietrich Bonhoeffer dealt with the problem of the Christian proclamation of the Old Testament, and he used a straightforward typology that is convincing in its simplicity.[34] It has often been referred to in the scholarly discussions in recent years. His point of departure is the statement that the whole Bible is the book of the Church.[35] The Bible is not only the record of the history of salvation, but Jesus Christ is also in the midst of it, in His low humanity and not in high religiosity.[36] The Old Testament has to be interpreted from its end and goal backwards, as well as in the forward direction in the line of expectation, which is the reason why Bonhoeffer can say, "He who desires to think and feel in terms of the New Testament too quickly and too directly is in my opinion no Christian."[37] The Old Testament drives man to an honest understanding of the "this-worldliness" of our life

[33] *Interpretation*, Vol. XII, July 1958. A much more detailed elaboration of the hermeneutical problem can be found in H. W. Wolff's article, "Zur Hermeneutik des Alten Testaments," *Evangelische Theologie*, Vol. XVI, 1956, pp. 337-370; the same issue of that journal contains more articles on the subject by various authors, partly in reply to the book *Die christliche Kirche und das Alte Testament*, by A. A. van Ruler of Utrecht, which has been the subject of hot debates. It is to be hoped that the whole complex of these essays and books will soon be translated into English.

[34] Cf. *Prisoner for God*, pp. 124, 153 ff., and more quotations in an essay by R. Grunow on Bonhoeffer's hermeneutics in *Die mündige Welt*, Vol. I (Munich: Chr. Kaiser Verlag, 1955), pp. 62 ff.

[35] Cf. *Creation and Fall* (London: SCM Press, 1959), p. 8.

[36] Cf. pp. 47 ff. on the worldliness of the Word.

[37] *Prisoner for God*, p. 79, (the translation there is different; this one is taken from *Interpretation*, *op. cit.*).

which, nevertheless, demands fulfillment. In that sense, all parts of the Old Testament bear witness to Christ, be it that they expect the Messiah or that they do not express any hope and do not see the way of forgiveness. The Old Testament protects the Christian proclamation against "false historicism," to use H. W. Wolff's terms,[38] which can be taken as a true elaboration of what Bonhoeffer intended to say but was unable fully to express before his death. The Old Testament in itself only has a meaningful existence and can meaningfully be interpreted only because of Jesus Christ, without whom the promise of God to Israel would be a perfect lie. The interpretation and the preaching of the Old Testament need not try to find ways to "smuggle" Christ into the texts, because He is already there. He is present in the priestly and prophetic words, and He is also present in the human words of the Psalms, because He is true man, born of the virgin Mary, because He intercedes for sinners, and stands vicariously for all men before God. We receive not only the priestly and prophetic words, but also the words of human response, from the hands of Jesus Christ Himself.

The underlying thought of this conception is undoubtedly the doctrine of the Trinity. The continuity between the old and the new Covenants, between yesterday and today, is not the faith of man, which has found its expression in the texts, but God Himself, Yahweh, who is the Father of Jesus Christ. It is only from that point of view that we can understand the single texts, which must then, of course, be interpreted faithfully and with all the tools of historical and linguistic study. No rules can be given, for each text must be allowed to speak its own witness.

The necessity of these thoughts on typology which we have summarized (with special emphasis on H. W. Wolff and Dietrich Bonhoeffer's understanding), can be shown by the problem raised in the simple question: Why do we still read the Old Testament? Surely it is not satisfactory merely to refer to the fact that the Old Testament is the historical basis of the New, or that the Old Testament was the Bible of Jesus and of the

[38] H. W. Wolff, *Evangelische Theologie,* Vol. XVI, 1956, pp. 360 ff.

Early Church. Granting these reasons, neither is the main reason. The real answer to the question is given in Romans 9-11, particularly in chapter 11 which says that the Church is ingrafted into Israel. The Gentile Christians live from the holy root of Israel (Romans 11:18), and their justification is totally based on the faithfulness of God in His promise to Israel. The Church has not adopted the Old Testament, but the Church has been ingrafted into Israel, whose Messiah is the Jew, Jesus. The false idea that Christ must be "taken into" the Old Testament is in fact identical with the statement that there are two Gods, one for the Jews (whose time is over), and one for the Church that adores a Lord who is accidentally a Jew. It is for this reason that the Church, by mistake, got interested in the Old Testament. This nonsensical thought has sometimes found supporters in the history of the Church.

If one considers the new emphasis of the studies in the "traditions" of Israel[39] as a response to God, one can perhaps count three possible approaches to the task of preaching Old Testament texts:

a. The kind of typology that is limited to certain *typoi*, i.e., types such as the priestly functions, David and the kingship, the sacrifices, the Temple, the feasts, election, etc., but especially to those *typoi* which are used in the New Testament, e.g., Melchizedek, the flood, the exodus, the patriarchs, etc.

b. The kind of typology that goes beyond certain *typoi* and takes the whole of the Old Testament (and the New, which includes passages that might cause difficulties for "Christological" preaching) as the book of the Church in such a way that the Trinitarian creed dominates and enables the preacher to approach his text Christologically right from the beginning. He sees (with Paul and others) Christ living in the old Covenant, but he can still be honest with his text and can still preach a "one-sided" sermon. The simple fact that he is preaching in

[39] Cf. pp. 41 ff., the references to James Barr's articles, which represent a discussion with recent research in the question of traditions and the history of their transmission (Martin Noth, etc.).

the Church enables him to speak of Christ and Gethsemane when he is preaching on Genesis 32 (Jacob's wrestling with the angel). But he feels in no way compelled to say that the authors of this tradition in Genesis 32 were thinking of Christ, since he knows perfectly well that they were not, and he will say this in his sermon. The same approach is possible with regard to passages which are far more remote from being *typoi*, e.g., verses from Proverbs or Ecclesiastes.

c. The careful decision not to think typologically and not to use the categories of prefiguration and analogy, but to take the human response which is found in the traditions very seriously so that the preacher might refrain from mentioning the name of Christ, if he thinks this to be necessary because of the text. The hidden presupposition of this conception is, of course, quite similar to a. and b.; otherwise there would be no difference from a synagogue sermon. But the difference is just that the election of Israel is seen to be fulfilled in Jesus Christ, so that the human words of response receive their meaning from that fact.

These three conceptions are, of course, not mutually exclusive. Combinations are possible, and different texts will require different approaches. Nevertheless, it can be observed that few preachers use all three methods. Perhaps it can be said that the first method proceeds from the promise to the fulfillment, thus following the intent of the text; that the second method proceeds from the fulfillment to the promise, thus seeing in retrospect how God has acted with His people; and that the third method tries to avoid using these aspects as presuppositions, thus attempting to leave it to the self-witness of the text itself to present the promise and the fulfillment. It would not be wise to evaluate these conceptions prematurely. They all represent rather different theologies, and it will be the task of each preacher to find his own way and to be ready to change his method through careful study.

Besides a great variety of unfortunate and false methods of preaching the Old Testament,[40] a rather practical or technical

---

[40] E.g., the allegorical method (which is difficult to define), in which there

approach can be mentioned in addition to the three basic theological ways: to use the last minutes of the sermon simply for
going beyond the text, in order to make a Christological *"finale."*
This is done either by drawing the line of the text much further
(which is a kind of typology), or by an abrupt break and a
new start, thus adding to the text "what the Church believes."
For that purpose, many preachers base their sermon on two
texts,[41] which they read together before the sermon begins.
One text is taken from the Old Testament, the other from the
New. Many jokes have been made in theological circles about
this effort to conclude the sermon with a glorious Christology.
It is certainly true that this should not be considered the ideal
method. However, there are no binding methods, in the first
place, and secondly it must be admitted that this Christological
preaching, which interferes with the self-witness of the Old
Testament text, is still much better than topical preaching or a
kind of interpretation that cannot see beyond the limits of
moralism or legalism, with which one is often confronted if a
text is taken at face value.

It must be said in conclusion that the mere mentioning of the
name of Jesus Christ is no guarantee that His name has really
been preached. It is indeed possible that the Incarnation, the
Cross, and Easter have been preached without verbal reference
to Jesus Christ. The constant repetition of His name, and general
reference to "the Gospel," "the forgiveness of sins," "salvation,"
etc., can be extremely meaningless — for all their orthodoxy.

---

is a disregard of the context and the molding of the traditions; or the
treatment of the Old Testament as a book of sacred moral codes, or as an
early stage of "progressive revelation," etc.

[41] The selection of two or three groups of verses within one chapter or
group of chapters is sometimes inevitable when preaching Old Testament
texts, for the texts are normally much longer than a New Testament pericope. The length can create some technical difficulties for the public reading before the sermon. This fact supports the value of the "one-sided"
sermon, for it is obvious that a verse-by-verse sermon is almost impossible
if the text has more than 20 or 30 verses. The selection of the parts of the
total passage is a highly responsible undertaking, and it can only be done
after careful exegetical work.

In many ways it is a sign of real trust in the power of the Word to allow an Old Testament passage to proclaim what forgiveness is, without going into outspoken Christology. A straightforward sermon on 2 Samuel 12 is "Christological," when it reaches its climax in verse 13: "David said to Nathan, 'I have sinned against the LORD.' And Nathan said to David, 'The LORD also has put away your sin; you shall not die.'" If one operates too quickly with Christological language and terms, many a message of the Old Testament can almost be made "relative." Nevertheless, the norm is not that the name of Christ is not mentioned in a sermon. If passages of the Old and the New Testaments are not self-explanatory in their form and language, one of the typological approaches will surely be in order. But again it is the text that must determine this, not a fixed typological method which the preacher tries to apply to all texts. It must also be seen that a certain approach may be used for one Sunday, but not for the whole year. This is another reminder not to think of the sermon as an isolated event.

7. THE UNION WITH CHRIST AND THE TWOFOLD APPROACH TO THE TECHNIQUE OF PREACHING

An authentic technique of preaching is determined by two criteria which are analogous to the promise that the Lord of the Church is both the call and the response. The technique of wording and delivering the sermon is primarily determined by the text and secondarily by the congregation which has shared the preacher's responsibility of proclamation. No two texts allow the same technique, and no two congregations either, even if the preacher preaches the same sermon in two churches on one Sunday.

The "Christological analogy," or (more concretely) the understanding that Jesus Christ, as true God and true man, is God's Word to us as well as our response to Him, has guided our considerations up to this point of the argument. There was no other way to strive for an understanding of Scripture and of the sermon. The sermon itself, as an event in and of the Church for the world, was conceived as the work of God the Father in His Son through the Holy Spirit, so that the formulation was accepted as meaningful, that the sermon is the "*proprium* of the Holy Spirit." This is, of course, only a formula, and as such it is without much value. But it also indicates more than a formula or artificial construction: it points to the truth that the sermon is worship and prayer, adoration of God and creation of history through the will of God to make Himself known. In one word, the formula points to the working of God who mercifully uses the words of sinful men for His divine purpose. The *Vergegenwärtigung* of God's wonderful deeds (1 Peter 2:9), i.e., the "embodiment" of His life-giving Word, is what happens through the power of the Holy Spirit during the sermon. And this leads the Church into patience and hope until the day of fulfillment, when no more sermons will be preached.

The emphasis on the work of the Holy Spirit can open the way for a kind of spiritualism, if we are not on our guard and do not accept with all obedience the written witness of the Bible as the only source of our preaching. The humble acceptance of the Biblical witness is the clearest expression of the fact that the Church is not yet triumphant but is still living in this world, in which the news of the new world is contrary to man's thinking and is, therefore, found to be a "stumbling block."

The double aspect of Christ's being the Word, the demand, and the command of God, in addition to being the obedient response and fulfillment, protects the sermon from being an idealistic or religious speech that appeals to certain natural abilities of man. On the contrary, the Christian sermon is *ad hominem*, directed to man, with the understanding that the hearers are reconciled with God through the death of the one man Jesus Christ.

After having attempted to clarify all this, it must now finally be asked what implications all this has for the technique of preaching. The "technique" cannot possibly be something that is "added" to theological thinking, and that uses other sources than those which are constitutive for the theological understanding of the sermon. In other words, theological and technical thoughts about preaching are one and the same thing. True technique is not separated from exegesis and dogmatical thinking. This fact implies a twofold warning. First, it is not possible to treat the technical questions apart from the Biblical understanding, e.g., by referring to rhetoric, to the value of reading good novels, or to the experience of pastoral work during the week. Second, it is not legitimate to claim that the technical questions are unimportant, that the main point is only the preaching of the Good News, and that all the formal and technical questions do not matter because of the free work of the Holy Spirit. The first point is not seen and admitted by the pulpit heroes and "effective preachers"; the second point is overlooked by sectarians and by idealistic dogmaticians.

It seems that authentic technique is determined by two criteria which are analogous to the promise that the Lord of the Church is both the call and the response. The two approaches lead *ad absurdum* when isolated from one another.

The first understanding is the relation of the technique to the text itself. It has already been said that the tension of the text should also be the tension of the sermon, and that the directness or the indirectness of the appeal, command, or consolation within the text should also appear in the sermon. Some texts invite us to preach a very radical and personal appeal, while others demand a more careful and almost intellectual pondering of arguments. When it comes to the wording of the sentences of the sermon and to the delivery, one can even go a step further and say that the one-sided message of a text also demands a one-sided technique. A sermon on Genesis 32 (Jacob and the angel) should represent, even in the outward form of delivery and gestures, the dramatic tension involved, as well as the uncertainty that has come to us through several traditions which we can hardly reconstruct, and which we certainly have to face when we preach this text. The "puzzling" element of this text does not permit a crystal clear, systematic sermon, which is divided into schematic paragraphs that represent an obvious sequence of logical thoughts. A sermon on the first eleven verses of 1 Corinthians 12 (the grace gifts), however, demands a completely different technique. Is it not true that sermons on parts of Isaiah 6, Luke 2, John 3, and 1 Corinthians 13, require very different wording, techniques, and gestures? The questions of the structure and technical delivery of the sermon, including the rhetorical aspects, the using of the voice, the hands, and the whole body of the preacher grow out of the understanding of the message of the text. If the preacher has really lived with his text during the week, he will not artificially project himself into the role of the text, but he will, almost unconsciously, be a witness to the Word in just this form in which the text has overwhelmed him. Even the reading of the sermon text before the sermon is the beginning of the witnessing. No two texts can be read with the same "technique."

Against this understanding, the point can be made that the preacher who serves his sermon text so obediently may actually lose his own personality and maneuver himself into the role of an actor who changes from Sunday to Sunday to the great surprise of his congregation. He may give up his own self and copy slavishly the atmosphere of the Biblical text. Here is the danger that impersonal reproduction is substituted for the personal witness. The preacher will be tempted to use to the extreme this method in the same measure that he neglects to live with his people under the Word during the week. But the more he shares his text with his people, the more natural will his identification with the text be, when preaching on Sunday. He will then not feel the pressure to "underline" dramatically something which is quite strange and new to the congregation. His function as a witness will not have to be "brilliant," but it will be natural and understandable for the congregation. This first criterion for the technique leads automatically to the second one, without which it would be artificial and impersonal. The second criterion consists in the relation of the technique to the congregation. The Biblical writers themselves applied their message, which they had received from the tradition, to the actual situation of the congregation. They would not have agreed with the idealistic thesis that each sermon could be preached in any congregation.[42] Preachers who serve in more than one church each Sunday know that it is hardly possible to preach literally the same sermon in two places, even where the social, educational, and theological situation is very similar. How much more is this true when one travels with a sermon from one country to another! A sermon that can endure this treatment is a polished theological lecture rather than a sermon. Even if it were sometimes possible to preach almost the same sermon in two places, the preacher would inevitably change the way of delivery, his gestures, and tone of voice, but he would still feel that he were the slave of his sermon, rather than a keryx, a herald, who proclaimed the Word that is new every morning.

The second criterion for the technique is identical with what has already been said[43] about the sharing of the congregation in the responsibility of proclaiming the Word. The collaboration of the church is not so much a matter of the minister's knowledge of all the people in his church as it is primarily a knowledge from the other direction; the congregation will have to know their minister, and it is in many ways his initiative to make this possible. If he hid himself in his "office," he might gain a certain knowledge of his people, but this knowledge would not really help him for his sermon. This attitude might even lead to the dangerous extreme that he takes the "opinions" and the viewpoints of his parishioners so seriously that he can

[42] This is the danger of the work of guest preachers, and actually a good reason for saying that guest preachers should only teach. Each parish minister knows from experience the difficulties of preaching the first sermon after returning from vacations; all the good thoughts and plans which he might have collected in the meantime will not really help him to preach. It is therefore good for preachers to leave their church from time to time, precisely in order to see this.

[43] Cf. pp. 127 ff.

never see beyond his own pastoral experiences. The true preacher will not rely on his knowledge of the people, for he will have a certain "suspicion" of their ideas as well as his own. He might become blind and deaf to the Word of God if he were never to free himself from involvement in his pastoral work. Helping to prevent this is precisely the task of the congregation, who must know the duty of the preacher to hear and to proclaim the Word of God, but who need not necessarily share his analysis of the situation and of the feelings within the church. This genuine assistance of the congregation will facilitate making the Sunday sermon truly the beginning of all pastoral care and counseling.

The technique of preaching, therefore, is not only determined by the sermon text, but also by the congregation.[44] The relation to the text has priority, but the second criterion must not be overlooked. To criticize this second criterion by saying that it is psychological or anthropological, and should therefore not be applied, is in fact denying the incarnation of Christ and the union between Him and His Church. This union, however, is the point of departure as well as the end of all thinking about preaching and of all the sermons that are preached. It is this union that distinguishes the faith of the Church of Jesus Christ so radically from religions and ideologies of this world.

It is true that preaching is, humanly speaking, impossible. As it is performed by man, it is a lie about God because it cannot rely on any proofs and cannot force God to act or speak. "With men it is impossible, but not with God." For God gives Himself in Jesus Christ into the hands of men, so that the sermon is true and authoritative, and it calls the world out of darkness and death to life with the exalted Christ. This gift is given to the whole Church for its service in the world.

[44] Tillich intends to express this with his method of "correlation," but I do not think that his approach is in any way unique. There was scarcely a good theologian in the history of the Church who did not employ a method of correlation! Tillich's method seems even less helpful than other methods, since it is based on a polarity of "question" and "answer" (e.g., *Systematic Theology*, Vol. II, p. 15), which, in my opinion, unduly systematizes the concreteness of man's situation. Would not the polarity "task-ability" be more realistic? Jeremiah, for instance, was not driven by a question, but by a task or by a commission.

Appendix

The intention of this book has been to refrain from giving methodological advice, except in those cases where concrete suggestions seemed to grow out of the Biblical and dogmatical conceptions. The Church would be very poor if it adopted a fixed method of preaching and of practical theology in the widest sense. There is no ideal method of preaching, and books that attempt to suggest one are rather like newspapers, which are interesting today but not tomorrow. With regard to the question of method, however, this genuine relativity by no means permits the idea that the whole question of the understanding of preaching as such is relative. Preaching is a highly theological problem, and in a way the center of all theology. The following discussion emerges from this conviction, as a response to seminary students and young ministers who have requested practical guide lines for finding theological integrity in their work of sermon preparation.[1]

Ministers who have studied theology in seminary, and then neglect their daily theological work during the years of their service in the Church, are precisely like physicians who hold a degree in medicine and yet do not pursue the questions of medicine any further, but behave as if they were nurses whose primary concern is practical work, efficiency, and a good bedside manner. No one would like to consult such a doctor; in fact he could be sued for malpractice. If a doctor is not allowed to forget his anatomy and all the other disciplines, why does a minister get by who does not care for solid theological work

[1] Ernst Fuchs, an exponent of a different theology from that which has been posited in this present book, reprints an excellent letter and summary statement on preaching and sermon preparation at the end of his remarkable book *Zum hermeneutischen Problem in der Theologie* (Tübingen: J. C. B. Mohr, 1959), pp. 345 ff. It is to be hoped that Fuchs' book will sometime be made available in English translation.

(including the Biblical languages!) after he has received his degree? Is his work less important? Are fifty-two sermons to hundreds of people a small matter? Or is the work of the Holy Spirit an excuse for being lazy and scientifically dishonest? If we do not change, the Lord of the Church may very well take away from us our seminaries, professors, and books and put our ministers in prison (as He has already begun to do in many parts of the world). Then there will be much lamenting and we will blame the powers of the world for it, instead of seeing that it is the judgment we deserve.

It may be permissible, in conclusion, to add some concrete and rather specific considerations, with regard to the preacher himself and to his sermon. This is done in the awareness that practical tasks can hardly be described in a book, but that they should rather be discussed[2] without being written, and then performed.

The primary task is the rediscovery of exegesis. Those parts of the Church and those ministers who read the Bible merely as a devotional book, as one might read in one's hymnbook, will die, and one will not have to regret that death. "Exegesis" cannot be the once and for all essay which the theological student has to write in his senior year. Exegesis is the preacher's weekly work, or else he is not a faithful minister. Each minister, however, has to find his solution to the problem created by the almost impossible balance between the four important factors in his life: his theology, his congregation, his health, and his family. Only a very disciplined man can try to master the problem, and even he will never really succeed. A hopeful effort is the attempt to combine the theological and the congregational work, so that there is an intimate connection between the exegetical and historical work and reading, and the practical usage

[2] It is an important task for the future to reach a new understanding of the brotherhood of the ministers, who study and pray together, exchange and criticize sermons, and subject themselves to a discipline, thus departing from the practical congregationalism which dominates in most of the Protestant denominations.

of certain passages and certain theological questions in the work of the church during the month. It is of great help to concentrate during a month on only one book of the Bible and on only one particular question in the field of ethics, or dogmatics, or history. No one can master the task of changing from one text and one question to the other, without giving up all serious theological work that grows out of those texts and questions. The exegesis of the sermon text should not require more than two to four hours (it then depends on the individual how much time will be needed for the preparation of the actual sermon). Here is a rather pragmatic suggestion as to how this can be done technically: one should write down the Hebrew or Greek text on a sheet of paper; key passages should be memorized; key words should be looked up in the concordance and in a dictionary; if they have many meanings, one will consult a book on Old or New Testament theology; historical and geographical details will be checked; cross references will be compared; hidden and obvious Old Testament quotations within the New will be looked up in the Septuagint and in the Hebrew; finally, an English translation will be made and written down. All this is often not very exciting, but it must be done. Only then is it possible to begin to "think" about the passage, and commentaries can perhaps be of help, although it is certainly possible to preach a sermon without having used a commentary. Commentaries are time consuming, since more than one must be used to avoid depending on an isolated opinion. If there are no commentaries by the early fathers available, the Reformers should be consulted and then one or two new commentaries. Commentaries should never be read at the expense of proper exegesis. Whether they are used or not, the next step is the investigation of the context, both the immediately preceding and the following chapters, and the context within the whole book. Now the specific passage with all its words and sentences is opened up. This concludes the actual "exegesis," and the time of prayer and careful listening begins.[3] It can extend over the time of many days and cannot be done in isolation from the congregation.

Another important task of the preacher is his critical attitude to journals, pamphlets, and books, and to opinions, ideas, and suggestions in general. It ought to be difficult to persuade a minister to read a journal or a book which is not already on his "list." Far too many books and articles are being read now; it is no wonder that the parish minister complains that he has no time for study, because he does not have a disciplined attitude to written material. A minister will hardly have more than three hours a day for the preparatory work of classes and sermons, and he cannot afford to read popular commentaries and pseudo-theological books, except for the purpose of knowing what he can recommend to the people in his church. He should also have some spare time for books which have not grown out of the Christian Church, although he will not read "the classics" and modern novels in order to be a "better preacher," but simply in order to be a well-educated man and to enjoy those books. In one word: the minister is free to feel and to behave as a man who has studied his field of theology with all academic humility and honor; he need not envy doctors, psychologists, sociologists, or businessmen with the hidden intention of being all of them in one person. He must not apologize for being a theologian, and least of all will he respect a fellow minister who says proudly that he is "no theologian" or is not interested in theology.

Still another task of the preacher is the examination of his attitude toward his own denomination and its tradition. Could not a strongly Reformed or Lutheran emphasis be very helpful to achieve the "one-sidedness" of the sermon that has been advocated in this present book? One can only agree here in

[3] "Finally we must close all our books and go back and wrestle with the text alone. One cannot preach from commentaries. . . . they cannot replace our own wrestling with the text as we try to hear God speaking to us where we stand." Paul M. van Buren, Anglican Theological Review, October 1957, pp. 356-357; cf. my reference on p. 50 above.

a very limited way. The denomination to which a Christian belongs is in many ways a matter of tradition and not so much the result of theological knowledge and faith. Only very few church members and not very many ministers could explain offhand the difference between Lutheran and Reformed Christology, or between Episcopal and Reformed understanding of the offices, without first looking it up in a textbook. Are those preachers therefore poorer preachers? Perhaps, but it is unrealistic to expect all responsible people within the Church to know the precise differences between the Churches in the *Ecumene* and to give the reasons that they themselves belong to this and not to another Church. But if this is so, if they are not fully equipped in this respect, preachers should not too hastily sing the praises of their own denomination. The constant quoting of Calvin and Luther in the two respective denominations is an indication of provincialism, and moreover, it is surely not in accordance with the intentions of the Reformers. If, however, a preacher feels firmly grounded in the history of doctrine, he can in all confidence explain and defend his denomination, even in the sermon, if this seems necessary for a one-sided and clear interpretation. True ecumenicity is not achieved by giving up one's own tradition, but rather by rethinking it from its very roots, so that one sees that it is not the doctrine that creates the Church, but Jesus Christ. But it must also be seen that in our generation we have become the witnesses of far deeper splits within the Church than those which were constituted by the theologies of the sixteenth century. We have to be on our guard not to minimize the new dangers of disunity which have broken into the Church with enormous power. The time is already approaching when it will no longer really be interesting whether a preacher is Reformed, or Methodist, or Episcopalian, but when everything depends upon whether or not he understands and preaches that the Good News of God in Jesus Christ can under no circumstances be confused with the culture in which we live.

Finally, reference has to be made to the much discussed

question of what the preacher should think about the intellectual and emotional ability of the congregation to understand the sermon. It is probably humanly impossible ever to preach an "understandable" sermon. Even if the preacher knew all the members of his church intimately, and even if he were a master in exegesis and in preaching, he could never force Jesus Christ to deal with the people, so that, "when they heard this they were cut to the heart." (Acts 2:37.) Perhaps it is even false to claim to preach "understandably." Certainly preaching should not be deliberately unintelligible, for 1 Corinthians 14:15 warns us: "I will pray with the spirit and I will pray with the mind also; I will sing with the spirit and I will sing with the mind also." The sharing of the congregation in the minister's responsibility, i.e., the corporate ministry, must not be taken as an invitation to the democratic ideal, so that everything should immediately be understood by everyone. A logical sequence of the sentences in the sermon is surely indispensable, but this is not identical with understanding. The prophets in the Old Testament should be taken as the clearest example of this, and many a preacher can add his own experience at this point. One can hear and keep in mind something which one does not understand at the moment. Those sermons which have "impressed" us most and have changed our lives most drastically were often fully understood only much later. A preacher can confidently think of this and must not strive nervously toward the ideal that each member understands immediately what the sermon says. Premature understanding and acceptance of the message is often more dangerous than the alternative. Easily understood and over-simplified sentences can be wrongly taken as the real life-giving Word of God. The tendency in our present church life is not toward sermons which are too complicated, but toward those which are too limited in language, too simple, and too much a repetition and reconfirmation of what the people have already heard long ago. The danger of being misunderstood is certainly greater than the danger of not being understood. The preacher's true love for his people is not shown by the attempt to treat them like children who badly need a spiritual father who knows the answers to their questions. True love, without which preaching is hardly possible, looks at the hearers of the sermon as mature men and women who know how to think and act during the week; how to hate and how to love; how to earn money and how to spend money. And the preacher will know that these people, in all their sin and weakness, stand with him under the Cross. They are given to him to serve together with him, even if they do not know it.

Index of Names